Fake Smiles and Lasagna

Fake Smiles and Lasagna

one high school teacher, two Rwandan refugees, and a
three year journey of self-discovery

CHRISTINE JENKINS

In loving memory of Lucille A. Siauris
(1937-2011)

Prologue

"It's the butter girl," he said. A wide smile deepened the maze of wrinkles around his eyes. The friendly fellow, wearing a white polo shirt stretched over his belly, was referring to my ten-year-old daughter, Rachel, whose job at the Providence soup kitchen was to scoop butter onto plates of guests passing in line for a warm meal. It was July of 2006, and we had been volunteering every Wednesday during the summer for five years.

"God bless you," the man said as she plopped butter onto his baked potato, half of it landing on his pork chop. He didn't mind. How could he be angry with a girl whose thick blonde curls bulged under a hair net draped lazily over one eyebrow, her fingers swimming in adult-size plastic gloves?

Rachel's seven-year-old sister, Sydney, took brief turns handing out bread and pastry, but otherwise absorbed herself in a Harry Potter book. She'd occasionally look up as if studying a new species. I wondered what thoughts crossed her mind as hundreds of people, all ages, paraded by. I guessed she was sizing them up, imagining how they had landed themselves in this place. I didn't care that she wasn't as involved as Rachel. It wasn't her thing. Her passion was for the earth and animals, and it stemmed from some place deep inside her, some place I had nothing to do with.

Rachel was the reason my kids became involved with community service from a young age. When she was three, and Sydney was an infant I toted on my back, we had volunteered at a smaller soup kitchen. I wasn't trying to teach them the importance of helping others. We did it because I thought Rachel would enjoy it, and I was right, although her enthusiasm waned during her preteen years. Compassion was a trait Rachel came into the world with – one that emerged as soon as she could speak.

When she was in nursery school, one of her teachers said, "I love this girl! She noticed I wasn't feeling well today."

Big deal, I thought. That's just the way she is. Of course, I had no other toddlers to compare her to, so to me she was just *being Rachel.*

As parents, we like to pat ourselves on the back for our children's virtues, but I've come to believe that nature is more powerful than nurture in influencing one's personality. Anyone who thinks otherwise probably doesn't have kids.

Despite our ongoing involvement with the soup kitchen, we felt – *I felt* – oddly disconnected from the people we worked with, as well as those we served. There was something unsatisfying about giving my time anonymously. Maybe I was too selfish to forego recognition. Perhaps I was seeking something for myself that I wasn't finding at the soup kitchen. But what? A sense of purpose? Alleviation of guilt?

At the very least, I wanted that good feeling you get from having helped someone. I wasn't getting it, and I felt cheated. That didn't stop me from going through the motions every week. We arrived at ten o'clock sharp to help set up, and I smiled for three incessant hours, doling out food and friendly comments. I left exhausted and unfulfilled – and often frustrated with my kids. Sure, they were good sports and everyone loved the butter girl, but they didn't feel the need to paste fake smiles on their faces. As soon as hunger hit and energy fizzled out, their expressions screamed apathy and boredom, forcing me to muster even more good cheer lest I leave unfulfilled *and* embarrassed.

I eventually grasped the reality that, for whatever reason, this gig wasn't working for me. And it wasn't doing much for Sydney either. Maybe it was time to redirect our efforts.

Clarity tapped me on the shoulder one day when we were volunteering at the soup kitchen. One of the workers, a sturdy woman with a purposeful gait, wanted my attention. She had been there every week.

"Hey, Lady!" she yelled from across the dining room. Really? I'm known as "Lady?" I suddenly understood why this experience fell short of my expectations: It would have been nice if, after five years, *someone knew my name.*

About two years after the "Lady" incident, our family began talking about helping refugees. Rachel and I had read a couple of books about people who had come to the United States to flee dire circumstances. We learned that their difficulties didn't end once the refugees set foot on American soil. Instead, the emigrants faced a new set of challenges that involved navigating their way in a predominantly English-speaking country with a complicated welfare system and a peculiar set of social norms. Making coffee, getting a library card and opening a bank account were just a few of the tasks they'd accomplish in their first weeks.

"I wonder if refugees ever come to Providence," Rachel said one Friday evening. It was family movie night, and we had just watched *Lost Boys of Sudan*, a documentary about two young men who had come to the United States to escape poverty and violence. The endearing personalities of the boys in the film captivated Rachel.

"Good question," I said from the opposite end of the sofa, gathering my ash brown hair into a ponytail.

"That was an amazing story," my husband, Wayne, said as he cleared away the empty popcorn bowls. Sitting across from us in the unlit living room, Sydney went back to reading her novel.

"You would think everything would be fine once they came here, but that's not true, is it?" I said to Rachel. "They need help with everything – shopping, cooking with American ingredients, figuring out transportation – can you imagine?"

Rachel shook her head, wide-eyed.

"We could find out if they need volunteers to help refugees who settle in Providence, if any of them do," I said.

"We should do that," Rachel agreed. She stretched her long legs across the sofa and sipped her tea.

"They probably go to Boston," Wayne said from the

kitchen. I figured he was right and let go of all but a speck of hope that we'd be meeting refugees anytime soon.

The next day, I started my online research. That's when I discovered the Rhode Island International Institute Refugee Resettlement Program – located practically in our backyard.

I would commit to helping refugees with fixed notions of reward: a good feeling, sense of purpose, maybe a boost in self-esteem. What I'd actually receive I couldn't have anticipated: lessons about resilience, faith, and finding joy in unexpected places.

This is the story of the transformative power of unlikely friendships, and it begins at the International Institute.

PART I

The Coming Tide

1

Meeting Sonia and Eugene

"We did not know where we were going, but we had to cross the border. My younger brother was crying and he said, 'Help us, God. Help us.' After two days of sleeping outside, we crossed the border to Zambia. We lived in Zambia for two years in a refugee camp. Life was so difficult because we were young, didn't have money and we did not know how to speak the native language of Zambia. We lived there, and we believed that something good would happen to us no matter how hard the life was because we believed in God."
-Sonia's English class essay, 2012

Have you ever imagined what aspect of your personality could earn you a spot on a daytime talk show? My caption would read "guilt ridden, anxious control freak searching for purpose in all the wrong places." Who else lets anxiety ambush a perfectly good moment – in this case a drive with my family to the Rhode Island International Institute to discuss our role as volunteers.

My eyebrows creased as I looked at my taupe sports watch. On this sunny day in early July 2008, my bulky watch declared we were twenty minutes late for our two o'clock appointment at the Institute, though I can't remember why. I hated to be late, and I never was. Until I had kids. Don't get me wrong – I was rarely the early bird. But showing up late felt rude and made me anxious, so I avoided it. This became impossible when a sibling dispute or misplaced book could at any moment disrupt my family's forward momentum. A reasonable person would have adjusted her expectations to align with life's circumstances. I just got cranky.

I kicked off my Chacos and propped my feet on the dashboard. Elbows on my knees, I clasped my head and focused on my bright pink toenails like I was practicing Lamaze while holding a strange yoga pose.

Country music poured from the radio and I almost let loose a laugh when Wayne imitated Blake Shelton singing "Some Beach." My husband's even-keeled temperament and good nature partnered well with my roller coaster moods. A well-read liberal with southern charm, Wayne blended into the northeast landscape better than I did – and I was born here. He grew up in southern Alabama, just above the Florida panhandle and deep inside the Bible belt. His drama-free voice and off-color humor settled my nerves.

Rachel and Sydney, twelve and nine, were under the spell of a new adventure. They'd normally bury their heads in books while in the car, but instead they chatted and sang along to the music. Almost three years apart, Rachel and Sydney got along quite well – probably because they were so different. Rachel had the easygoing personality of a golden lab and Sydney the focus of a bloodhound.

Although strong willed, Sydney often sought Rachel's advice, especially when it came to important matters – like fashion choices. Determined to make a proper first impression at the Institute, they'd put considerable thought into their outfits. Rachel chose a "Save the Whales" jersey, and Sydney wore one of her many "Go Green" t-shirts. They weren't going to chance being denied the opportunity to help a refugee transition to their new life.

It took under twenty minutes to reach our destination, an imposing boxlike building set against a background of small businesses, empty lots and a street clotted with traffic lights. Its beige brick façade and scarcity of windows gave it a cold, unwelcoming appearance. We wouldn't have noticed the small entrance on the side if it hadn't been shaded by a vibrant blue awning, which stood out like a brightly colored buoy against a grey fog.

Just inside the door a receptionist appeared to be keeping guard, but with a nod she let us by. We descended a flight of stairs and filed down a hall, following signs to the refugee resettlement office.

There, another receptionist brought us through a maze of cubicles and introduced us to the director of the department, Babak Amiri. A short Iranian man with thick hair and a cleft palate, Babak spoke in a soft, slow voice. I expected someone more outgoing and less businesslike, as if extroversion was a requirement for social work – a silly assumption, coming from an introverted teacher with a degree in psychology. I tried not to be put off by his formality. After all, there was no reason for him to match my enthusiasm. I could only imagine the time and energy he poured into his job on a daily basis.

Babak stood with the four of us in front of a bulletin board covered with names of refugees who had recently arrived in Providence: an Iraqi couple with a small child, a thirty-year-old man from Sierra Leone, a brother and sister from Rwanda. I asked to hear more about the siblings. Babak explained that Sonia, nineteen, and Eugene, eighteen, had arrived two weeks earlier and were living on their own. Both parents were deceased. Their English was pretty good.

"What do you think, girls?" I said, as if asking them to choose an ice cream flavor. But my reticent girls weren't going to express an opinion, not in front of a stranger. Wayne shrugged, so the decision was mine.

"I understand if you need time to think before making a commitment," Babak said. The commitment was to spend one day a week for at least four months helping the new arrivals transition to North American culture.

"No, we don't need to think about it," I said with a stutter in my throat. "When can we meet Sonia and Eugene?"

"They're here now. Would you like me to introduce you to them?"

We thought we'd be discussing our role as volunteers that day. We had no idea we'd meet refugees. There were dozens of names on that bulletin board and I could have picked any of them. But I didn't. I chose Eugene and Sonia. The decision felt like one that would have a lasting effect on our lives.

There's something in mathematics called the butterfly effect. Simply put, it's the idea that a small change in an initial condition can have a profound effect on something down the road. The conflict in time travel stories is based on this concept: One small change in the past can significantly alter the future. That's how I felt about the moment we agreed to meet Sonia and Eugene. Picking a family from the bulletin board was a small event, but one that would have a lasting effect on our lives.

We, of course, agreed to meet Sonia and Eugene, so we followed Babak back down the hall and up the stairs. I matched my stride to his, with my family trailing behind. We hooked a left, down a short corridor that led to a large, open room. Round tables, snack machines, and a handful of people occupied the space. Poster-size photographs of refugees from faraway places decorated the walls. A smaller adjacent room accommodated a cooking class. We crept in to get a closer look.

A kitchenette in the back held long metal shelves overflowing with utensils, baking pans and ingredients. The ethnically diverse audience consisted of twelve students of varying ages spread out along five rectangular tables. All eyes followed the instructor: a young man, energetic and friendly, who gave slow, clear directions on how to make a Jiffy cake. A few students glanced at us. One woman, wearing a blue and yellow headscarf, was nursing her infant. She had high, exotic cheekbones, and I wondered if she realized how stunning she looked.

As I studied the constellation of students, the entire place began to whisper a new melody. This one resonated with me, pulled me in. I wanted to know more about what took place in this room, where these individuals came from. I wanted to know *their stories*.

Babak discreetly pointed out Eugene and Sonia to us, and I was surprised they weren't sitting together. Sonia sat at a table behind Eugene, and I would've guessed they were strangers. Eugene's chair was pulled away from the table, his legs spread casually, revealing a pair of loose navy shorts and milk-white basketball sneakers. Sonia compacted herself, as if she didn't want to take up too much space in the world. A yellow t-shirt hugged her narrow shoulders.

We waited outside the kitchen as Babak spoke with our soon-to-be friends and prepared them for our introduction. Moments later, the pair inched toward us, eyes not ready to meet ours. Eugene was shorter than I expected, sinewy with broad shoulders. Sonia was slightly taller, with a dainty waist. Her piercing chestnut eyes and delicate features conveyed a gentleness about her. I wondered what obstacles they had braved to get here.

Wayne, the gregarious one in our family, kept a low profile as though he wanted me to take the lead in establishing a relationship with Eugene and Sonia. Rachel and Sydney stood by my side with hands clasped below their waists, regarding the pair with somber curiosity. I'd been looking forward to this moment, but feared the wrong choice of words or body language would turn it sour. A smile fixed itself on my face in a floundering attempt to help Eugene and Sonia unbend. I found myself fast-forwarding in my mind to a time when I'd be closely connected to this pair, and the vast ocean between us would be evaporated. I would remember how it all flowed forward from this moment.

After brief introductions, I explained to Eugene and Sonia that I'd be picking them up the following week to spend time with them after their class. Of course, I had no idea what we'd be doing, but I'd figure that out later.

"Wednesday, right here after your class, OK?" I said with the pep of a kindergarten teacher. They nodded like obedient children, but the hesitation in Eugene's eyes made him appear confused and suspicious of our intent.

"See you next week," I said, offering my friendliest smile. Wayne shook their hands and the girls waved good-bye.

As our red Mazda pulled away from the parking lot, my eyes reexamined the building we had just left. It suddenly appeared strong and unpretentious, like those who stood within its walls. I couldn't wait to return.

2

Getting Acquainted

"I worried about how I was going to learn English. Some days I would take the bus to the Institute or somewhere else. I wasn't sure which bus to take or where to get off." -Eugene

I couldn't fathom what it was like for Eugene and Sonia to be plunked onto new soil like apples off a tree branch. With little education and no family for support, they had to find jobs, adjust to a new culture and communicate in a second language. The only experience I had to draw on, which provided me with almost no perspective, was when I quit my first full-time job after college and moved to a new city without a plan.

I was teaching at a boarding school in rural Pennsylvania, my existence shielded by matronly brick buildings set among three hundred acres of manicured playing fields and walkways. It didn't help that the small town of about a thousand people was cut off from the rest of the world by mountains and miles of farmland. I couldn't escape my professional role. This was most clear to me one night when I sat coiled under a tattered quilt in the unlit living room of my apartment in a boys' dormitory. I was clutching a Sam Adams Lager as if it were my only reminder that I was not defined exclusively by my teaching role. I was a real person, and I wanted to be left alone. I could hear the residents talking outside.

"I know she's in there. I saw her go in."

They kept knocking, but I wouldn't answer.

After what felt like an hour, the hallway was again quiet, but now I was trapped inside, committed to an evening of silence and darkness.

My only escape from this bubble of academia came in the form of unaffordable trips to Rochester, where my boyfriend was attending medical school.

So, with barely a carload of possessions and Lucas, my adopted Rhodesian Ridgeback, I moved to Rochester. Without a job. My relationship was not on solid ground by any means, although I naively thought it was.

Living with my boyfriend was not an option. His parents were paying his medical school tuition, and they didn't approve of me. I was, in their eyes, a distraction. That should've been a clue that he wasn't worth staying in town for – at least not without a real job.

There I was with Lucas, my barely furnished apartment, a college degree and one year of teaching on my resume. Although I managed to piece together part-time jobs to make ends meet, each month ended the same way: me curled up in the fetal position next to a pile of bills, checkbook in hand, sobbing. How was I going to get by? Where was my life heading? What was a cold-natured person like me doing this far north? This life was not what I had envisioned for myself.

Without a decided career path, I gave my self-esteem permission to take a nosedive. Socializing with ambitious medical students didn't help to reel it back in. Most importantly, I didn't have anyone nearby who really knew me. My relationship wasn't strong enough to shoulder my self-doubt. As it crumbled, I could feel my identity slipping away like the sand beneath my toes when I stand at ocean's edge. I was even becoming a stranger to myself. It's amazing how important it is to be known to *someone*. At that time, all my someone's seemed a million miles away.

The following week, the girls and I waited for Eugene and Sonia outside their classroom. Through the doorway, I watched them gather their notebooks and pens without looking at each other, or me. I wondered if they remembered our plan.

As they edged toward me, I asked them (in a voice three octaves higher than normal), "How are you?"

"Good," Sonia said.

"How was your class?" I said. Eugene looked puzzled like he didn't understand my question.

"Did you have a good class?" I repeated, this time enunciating every word.

"Oh, yes," Eugene said.

"What did you learn?"

Eugene looked at me like I had said something crazy.

"Can you tell me how to get to your house from here?" I asked him. I still couldn't read his face, so I looked at Sonia.

"Yes, I think so," she said.

They followed me to my car. Sonia sat in the front and directed me to their apartment several blocks away. Eugene, Rachel and Sydney filled the back seat with their silence. It felt like hours had passed by the time we pulled into their driveway.

The door to Eugene and Sonia's third-floor apartment opened to an oversized dining room. A scuffed ivory refrigerator stood prominently against the far wall, oddly separated from the adjacent kitchenette. A large table, covered with a burnt-orange cloth, occupied the opposite side of the room. Behind it, tall windows trimmed with peeling off-white paint overlooked the parking area, which took the place of a backyard. All other rooms connected to this space.

Sonia's room was the first one on the left, next to the bathroom. A blue and red comforter draped over her unmade bed; yellow sheets posed as curtains. Awaiting drawers and shelves, her clothes, lotion, a mirror, and scattered papers covered her dresser and the floor beside her bed.

On the other side of the dining room, a loveseat, two chairs and television crowded a bedroom-size den. Eugene and Sonia's roommate, Emmanuel, a quiet man who was also a refugee, occupied the next room. Adjacent to his room was Eugene's. Besides his bed and dresser, Eugene's room held a boom box, a backpack and a pair of basketball sneakers set in perfect alignment against the wall.

After the brief tour of the apartment, we returned to the dining room. To avoid another lapse into silence, I yanked out of my backpack a set of instructional English CDs and portable CD player that I had brought them. Eugene watched me curiously as I showed him how to use it. Sonia looked less interested. Her English was better than Eugene's.

"Your English is good, but this will help you get better," I explained to Eugene.

"Thank you," Eugene said.

"Did you study English in Africa?" I asked looking at Eugene, then Sonia. Rachel and Sydney sat on opposite sides of the table looking unimpressed.

"Yes, I studied in school," Sonia said. "I went to school longer than Eugene. He had to work. But my English is still not good."

"Your English is very good, Sonia. But you should both use this CD and these books," I encouraged. "Everything will be easier once you learn English." I looked at Eugene when I said this. He nodded, but I wasn't sure how much of the conversation he was following.

Sonia rattled something off in her native tongue, and Eugene responded, his voice strong and insistent. An intrigued Sydney finally perked up. Rachel's lips parted in surprise, showcasing her blue braces. She was caught off guard by Eugene's animated authority.

When they finished their private conversation, I asked lots of questions about their living situation. Sonia explained that the International Institute provided the apartment and a small amount of money for them to live on. They were expected to be self-supporting in three months, and someone from the Institute was helping them find jobs.

"I want to go to school," Eugene said clearly. "I want to go to high school."

"You will, I'm sure," I said automatically, but had no idea how or when that would happen.

Two weeks later, we again visited them in their apartment. It was the third day into a heat wave, and the air was packed with moisture. Sweat broke out on my forehead as I climbed the stairs to Sonia and Eugene's apartment, my two girls following my footsteps. Wearing shorts and a tank top, I toted a plastic grocery bag stuffed with eggs, bread, butter and cheese. The girls were more dressed up with skirts and flowery shirts. The balmy weather had convinced us all to wear our hair up.

I knocked on the door to Eugene and Sonia's apartment. There was no answer. Again, and still no answer. Was there a misunderstanding about when I was coming? I decided to call on my cell phone.

"Sonia, it's Chris. We're outside your door," I said into my phone.

"I'll be right there," she said as she opened the door. She was wearing a calf-length, silky jade dress that looked too fancy for hanging around the house. I wasn't sure where Sonia got her clothes, and I was careful not to ask too many questions. I had read online that it was considered rude in their culture to ask personal questions directly. I wasn't sure what that meant, but I didn't want to chance insulting her. I desperately wanted her to like us.

Sonia was alone; Eugene was playing soccer with his friend, Jean Pierre, who lived across the street.

"I brought you some fresh eggs from our chickens," I said and handed her the carton of mismatched eggs. Sonia opened the box and inspected them.

"What's the matter? Don't you like eggs?"

"Yes, I do," she said with a giggle that revealed a missing front tooth.

"Do they look the same as eggs you ate in Rwanda?" That may have been a stupid question, but I wondered why she studied them so intently.

"Yes, they're good," she said.

I unpacked my grocery bag. "We brought stuff to make grilled cheese sandwiches for lunch. Have you ever had grilled cheese sandwiches?"

"No."

"Oh, they're good, Sonia. You'll like them." Rachel said with a melody in her voice.

"OK." Sonia re-inspected the eggs before putting them in the refrigerator.

With her permission, I did a quick inventory of her cabinets: a few worn pots and pans, a bag of potatoes, a random assortment of glasses and plates, a can of Lysol and a Jiffy cake mix. She kept a fifty pound bag of rice next to her stove, which I expected would last them several years. I made a mental note to myself: Sonia needs baking pans, a colander, and some large utensils.

Sonia, Rachel and I crammed into the kitchenette while Sydney sat at the table wishing she had a book. If I let her, she'd read constantly – at the dinner table, in church, at parties. She once read in the shower. A plastic Ziploc bag protected her book and a hole in the bottom provided access for page turning. She looked lost without a book right now, and I almost wished she had one.

I took out a frying pan and melted some butter.

"What are you doing?" Rachel asked. "You're supposed to put the butter on the bread." I shot her my disapproving mother look.

"That's the way Grandma does it," she said. Grandma's way is not the only way, I thought.

"It doesn't matter. This way is easier," I replied. Rachel grimaced, and Sonia laughed at our exchange. I wondered what kind of relationship Sonia had had with her mother.

I thought of Eugene and Sonia's mother often when I first met them. Perhaps it was because I knew that my presence in their life and her absence were directly related. At times I could almost feel her watching over us, encouraging our relationship.

We spent a lot of time with Eugene and Sonia that first summer. Being a teacher afforded me that opportunity, and I was grateful. The frenzy of the school year would soon engulf me. I was determined to make the most of the unscheduled weeks on my calendar before they vanished.

I planned our visits to Eugene and Sonia's to be productive as well as social. I helped them open bank accounts and search for jobs, and I tried to equip them with basic household supplies. They never asked for anything but would offer a list when pressed. It was easy for us to get our hands on their list items. We simply had to ask around at church or school to find people willing to donate items they no longer needed.

Besides, I didn't like showing up empty-handed. I couldn't imagine they'd want to see me if I did. In fact, I approached my relationship with them like everything else in my life – strategically. Yup, I had a plan. I'd spend time with them, find out what they needed and help them as best I could, as cheerfully as I could – basically swoop in like Superwoman. To save them from what, I didn't know. In return, they'd like me, and I'd enjoy the good feeling of knowing I had impacted their lives. And we'd all live happily ever after. Not a bad plan, right?

Eugene wanted a computer and a bicycle. I explained to him that, even if he had a computer, he wouldn't have online access unless he paid for it. He wasn't in a position to do that yet. Still, I felt bad for not producing one of the few things he asked for.

Luckily, someone from the International Institute donated a bicycle to Eugene. Wayne and I took him to Walmart to get a new tire. The following week, while visiting Sonia and Eugene at their apartment, Eugene explained that he had another flat tire.

"So you need to go back to Walmart?" I tried not to sound

frustrated. Walmart was several miles from his house, and I hated city driving.

"No, I'm good," he said, "I went to Walmart with Jean Pierre."

I wondered how two boys, new to the area and with little English under their belt, had mastered the public transportation system so quickly.

"How did you know which bus to take?"

"We're smart," Eugene said.

Maybe I deserved that. Maybe I underestimated these boys.

"Yeah, we took the bus that said 'Walmart,'" he said, looking very pleased with himself.

Eugene was, in some ways, starting to remind me of my older brother, Joey. Both of them offered few details about their lives. When asked a question, they gave short, blunt answers, making conversation difficult. Also like my brother, Eugene would sometimes reply to my questions with sarcasm, as if to stop me from probing. It didn't bother me though, because I appreciated witty sarcasm as much as anyone. Besides, Eugene and my brother both had a way of delivering it with a playful tone, which I chose to interpret as affection.

I didn't think Eugene was any different with his sister. One would assume their shared plight would have shaped their relationship in unique and positive ways. I believe it did, though at first blush they appeared like any teenage siblings: They didn't talk to each other. Not much, anyway, as far as I could tell.

Occasionally, however, they'd engage in a lighthearted

conversation prompted by Eugene saying something outrageous, like he was going to join the army or move to Tennessee. If he was trying to ruffle his sister, he was unsuccessful. Giggling, Sonia would challenge his assertions while Eugene remained visibly unamused.

One time, I unintentionally managed to make them both laugh out loud. I had found a Kinyarwanda/English dictionary online. I practiced saying, "Amakuru yawe?" (How are you?) until I was satisfied with my pronunciation. I was excited to surprise them, not only with what I had found, but also with my ability to say something in their native language.

Then one afternoon, as the girls and I sat with Sonia and Eugene at their dining room table, I prepared our friends to be impressed, explaining what I had found. I uttered the greeting with smooth confidence, in proud anticipation of their delight. Increasing my volume with each pronunciation, I repeated the phrase in an effort to erase their blank stares. When I finally told them what I was trying to say, as if I had flipped a switch, their confused expressions turned to infectious laughter. Even when they corrected me, I couldn't detect the subtle difference in their pronunciation. Nonetheless, to their ears I had managed to make an ordinary word unintelligible.

Although the laughter was at my expense, I felt a great sense of accomplishment in making Eugene's face light up. It was a rare treat. He was hard to read, but I was determined to strip away his armor.

After practicing several words in Kinyarwanda, I helped

Eugene complete an application for a Social Security card. He came out of his room with what looked like a heap of papers he'd retrieved from the garbage. The control freak inside me wanted to scream. No worries, I told myself. I'd bring file folders next time.

Eugene and Sonia weren't used to having so many documents to keep track of. In fact, they were surprised by some of the bills they had to pay, like the water bill. Organization was my go-to remedy for anxiety, so that was my solution for them as well. I helped them label their file folders and sort and categorize their bills, bank statements and miscellaneous papers. I wrote on their calendar the days I would be visiting. I didn't want there to be any confusion.

I remained connected to the International Institute for several months after meeting Sonia and Eugene. I learned that they provided financial support for three to four months, but they wouldn't cut anyone off if they weren't yet employed. The Institute received money from the government and donors and relied heavily on volunteers. I attended a couple of orientation sessions for mentors in hopes of learning how best to help Eugene and Sonia. I had so many questions. What if they got sick? Did they have medical insurance? What if they couldn't afford to pay their bills or buy groceries? I felt as qualified for the position I had assumed as I was to perform infant heart surgery – and sorry for Sonia and Eugene whose ill luck had fated me as their mentor.

And as fate would have it, Sonia did get sick that summer.

It was a night we had planned to take her, Eugene and Jean Pierre to the WaterFire festival in downtown Providence.

Several weekends each summer, thousands of visitors flocked to see the floating bonfires along the river in downtown Providence. Meditative music resounded from speakers along the riverbanks. Alongside tourist-filled gondolas, black-clad volunteers scurried along in boats to feed the flames. Visitors looked on, mesmerized by the combination of sight and sound. Those who strayed from the river stumbled upon street entertainers, Del's lemonade trucks and kettle corn stands.

Wayne and the girls loved WaterFire festivals. I, however, would rather have had my eyelashes plucked out one by one than be near a crowd that size. Wandering through a sea of people, trying not to lose family members along the way, only to catch an occasional glimpse of fire on water, did not rank high on my list of fun things to do. But I thought Eugene and Sonia might enjoy it. Besides, it was close to their house, and it was free.

The night was oppressively warm. The fans in Eugene and Sonia's apartment did little to cut the thick air. It was only a week earlier that I had been in their apartment assembling the fans with Sonia, giggling as we tried to decipher the instructions. Sonia had surprised me that day by making a Jiffy cake.

The mood tonight was much heavier. Sonia lay in her bed exhausted and uncomfortable. After a quick check of her symptoms, Wayne drove to the drugstore to buy Nyquil and throat lozenges. I tried to convince Sonia to come to my house for the night where she could sleep comfortably in an air-conditioned room. She insisted on staying put.

"Are you sure, Sonia? We can bring you back tomorrow," I said.

"No, I'll be fine," she replied in a tiny voice. An ivory sheet covered the bottom half of her body.

It saddened me to leave her alone, but I understood why Sonia didn't want to come to my house. I was, after all, a stranger to her. Her bedroom, with peeling paint and bare walls, was her new home. And home is the only place you want to be when you're sick.

By the time Wayne returned, Eugene and Jean Pierre were eager to get going. Eugene had been out all day with Jean Pierre and barely noticed his sister had fallen ill. Wayne felt compelled to say something.

"Eugene, Sonia's not feeling well," he began. They were standing in the parking lot waiting for me to come down from the apartment. Eugene's fingers were pushed deep inside the pockets of his loose shorts. "Look, Eugene, Sonia is the only family you have here. You need to look after each other." Wayne's friendly face didn't match his serious tone.

I would have thought those words could have gone without saying. My mind didn't rush to judgment though. I figured there was an explanation, maybe something from their past or a difference in their culture. From an outsider's viewpoint, it seemed more reasonable that their situation would tighten their bond. Maybe it did, but all observable clues suggested otherwise. Something just didn't add up, and my curious mind couldn't stop theorizing.

As I headed down the stairs, Eugene ran back to say something to his sister. We never asked what it was.

It wasn't until three years into our relationship that Sonia filled in the missing pieces for me – their experiences before I met them, their vision of American life, their difficult transition. So much of what I observed between Sonia and Eugene made sense after she shared these bits; it only makes sense that I share them as well.

3

Before Our Paths Crossed: Sonia and Eugene

"I wasn't happy (when I arrived at the airport) because the people who came to pick me up, they were all black. In my mind, I was thinking that it was time to meet some white people and there weren't any. I was kind of disappointed at that point." -Sonia

Miniature houses grew life-size as the Boeing 737 descended toward stretched pavement. Eugene fidgeted with the emergency landing card. Sonia prayed. They wondered where they were. They knew they were in the United States – some place called Rhode Island – but that held no meaning for these teenagers, far from the grassy hills and clay houses of Rwanda.

The country they fled remained in critical condition fourteen years after the Rwandan genocide. Over 800,000 men, women and children were brutally murdered during the one hundred days of bloodshed that began in April, 1994. Whole villages were destroyed. Women were raped and children massacred with machetes. Mass burials marked with wooden crosses standing tall in perfect rows served as reminders of the violence that decimated the small country.

Laughter, love and the protection of seven older brothers filled Eugene and Sonia's childhood before the war. They lived in a plain but comfortable home in a peaceful neighborhood where children made soccer balls from trash and homemade twine, explored the grassy hills without fear or supervision.

Life was good.

Eugene and Sonia were four and five when the war began. The genocide claimed the lives of both their parents and at least four of their brothers. (Two were forced into hiding and never found.)

After her husband was killed, Sonia and Eugene's mother kept the family together as best she could, risking her own life at times for their safety. Though years muddied their memories, Sonia could recall standing vigil by her mother's bedside for nearly thirty hours before a fatal wound took her life. A heaviness descended on Sonia as she searched her mind for the right words to inform and comfort her younger brother.

Sonia was only a year older than Eugene, but she wore a maternal role with him – a role forced upon her during the war. To escape the hands of encroaching guerrillas, Sonia and Eugene's family would scatter and hide in the bush. Sonia's job was to stay with her youngest brother, to keep him safe. So when her mother died, Sonia was determined to stay strong for Eugene. It's what her mother would have wanted.

The siblings passed the years following their mother's death in refugee camps and under the care of an aunt who eventually abandoned them. But not before she paved the way for them to come to the United States as refugees. With the help of a neighbor, their prayers were eventually answered when they received word they'd be coming to the U.S., a place they'd heard was overflowing with wealth and opportunity. Ripe fruit dangling from trees, upscale apartments fully furnished, modern schools with passionate teachers – this was the America that lived in their imaginations. They pictured themselves eating scrumptious meals on their plush sofa, going to school, making many friends. Sure, they'd get jobs, eventually – once they had their degrees. Until then, they'd focus on their education. Yes, it was scary to start over in a new country, but the siblings never doubted they'd have a good life.

Sonia and Eugene shuffled through a windowless walkway and descended an escalator leading to the baggage claim area, gripping plastic bags decorated with prominent blue letters: UN. This was their only identification.

Many pairs of eyes looked up from the bottom of the escalator, and the siblings scanned the sea of faces for a glimmer of acknowledgment. A dark-skinned woman in a colorful loose dress emerged. As if she knew them, she nudged her way toward Eugene and Sonia and embraced them. Sonia noticed a slight limp, but the woman's eyes, filled with strength and compassion, soothed their spirits.

"Murakaza neza muri Amerika," the woman said, greeting them in their native language. She introduced herself as Annet, then directed them to the baggage carousel. Annet was a volunteer who had come to the U.S. as a refugee a few years earlier. She kept track of arrivals from her home country so she could welcome them at the airport.

Three black men from the International Institute stepped forward, helped them gather their luggage and led Sonia and Eugene to a car parked in a lot across the street. Before they knew it, Annet had vanished without saying "good-bye."

The sun was high in the sky but the cool breeze meant it wasn't quite summer. The New England June weather wasn't that different from Zambia's, where the siblings had spent the last three years. The men loaded the bags into the trunk. Eugene and Sonia sat in the back seat without uttering a word.

It was a short drive, maybe twenty minutes, to their new home – a third-floor apartment in a congested residential neighborhood abutting a busy commercial district. Comforting smells of fried potatoes and curry greeted them as they neared the third-floor landing. Annet and several other women busied themselves in Eugene and Sonia's kitchen, preparing a traditional African meal. The apartment was nothing special, but the familiar language and aromas gave the space a homey feel. Around the oversized kitchen table, they scarfed down generous portions of potatoes, chicken and collard greens.

Sonia studied her new home and the friendly strangers in her dining room. She leaned on her senses for clues and comfort. Eugene kept his eyes on his plate. He was happy to be fed, and the women were friendly enough. But Eugene was not impressed with his new home. The dingy apartment with scuffed appliances and mismatched furniture was a far cry from the fancy homes he had seen in pictures. The neighborhood, the apartment, the people – everything was different from the paradise he had painted in his mind.

After dinner the women shared stories with Sonia and Eugene, encouraging them to do the same. Sonia mentioned the name of her aunt in Zambia who had been taking care of her and Eugene after their mother died, and Annet said she knew the aunt. This comforted Sonia, who had forgiven her aunt for abandoning her and Eugene to live with a relative in Germany. Eugene bristled at the mention of her name.

"You can't stay here, alone, on your first day," Annet said in Kinyarwanda. "You will come with me to my house and meet my family."

That evening, as Eugene and Sonia sat in Annet's modest living room, they began to let go of their preconceived notions of America, and recalibrate their expectations. They suddenly had much to take in. For Sonia, this included Annet's twenty-three year old brother, Robert, a sharply dressed man whose sophisticated manner complemented his pleasant demeanor and easy laugh. Sonia was taken with him immediately. But she pushed her feelings aside, vowed to focus on her own life before getting involved with someone.

Improving her English and furthering her education would be her pursuits.

Later that night, in their unadorned apartment, the weight of loneliness settled on Sonia and Eugene. But it didn't foil their resolve to make a good life for themselves. They made a pact to wait until they were thirty before either of them married. They had much to accomplish, and they didn't need the distraction of a relationship to get in their way.

Over the next few weeks, Robert helped the pair transition to U.S. culture, and he made daily visits to their apartment. By many accounts, Eugene and Sonia were fortunate – fortunate to be alive, fortunate to be in the United States, fortunate to have Annet's family to help them. Life would be easy now that they were safe and opportunity surrounded them. At least that's what they thought *before* they landed on American soil.

Loneliness and sibling discord were not the least of the challenges Eugene and Sonia faced their first weeks in Providence. Although Robert offered support to both siblings, Eugene didn't like the new stranger paying attention to his sister. Sonia had never had a boyfriend, and her brothers had always protected her. Eugene didn't trust Robert, and he told him so with his snarky looks and unfriendly behavior. He broadcast his disapproval to Sonia with his stubborn silence and disappearing acts.

So there they were – two parentless teenagers, seven thousand miles from home, with no family to support them. And they were as pissed off at each other as any typical pair of American siblings. They needed a parent, a full time social worker and a miracle maker. They would get none of these. Instead, a white woman with a family, a full-time job and an assortment of anxieties would plop herself into their lives.

That woman, of course, was me, and I couldn't even point to Zambia on a map. How would we ever find common ground?

4

Before Our Paths Crossed: Chris

The anxious control freak I described earlier (remember, the one who couldn't stand to be late?) didn't always reign over my psyche. Everyone has different shades to their personality, don't they? I, for one, love an adventure, especially one that throws me clear of my comfort zone. Close friends have described me as goofy. The lens of middle age brings these contrasts into razor-sharp focus, and helps me appreciate the times when I'm not guarded or acutely aware of the passing hours. For me, those moments reside mostly in my childhood. At the beach. And at my grandparents' house.

My grandparents, Mémère and Pépère, had lived in central Massachusetts on top of a hill. Their quarter-mile dirt driveway, which became a death slide after a snowstorm, separated them from suburban life below. Their world, *our world*, consisted of strawberry patches, wooden forts, beagles, chickens and a blueberry-filled forest. It was the perfect playground. There, time disappeared.

I spent many weekend afternoons meandering through the woods behind my grandparents' house in search of the perfect blueberry bush – dense with ripe, plump fruit. My cousin and I would pluck the blueberries one by one, drop them into our plastic bowls and watch them accumulate. It was as if we were depositing gold coins into a piggy bank, to be cashed in only when we'd gathered enough to realize our highest aspirations.

Because time had no import on the hill, my cousin and I were not deterred by the adults' response when we showed them the fruits of our patience.

"Is this enough for a blueberry pie?" I'd ask, standing in my grandparents' basement kitchen, which looked like a cozy, cluttered dungeon.

"No, not quite," my mother would answer, Mémère watching in amusement.

"You may have enough for something else, muffins maybe," Mémère would suggest as she stood by the farmhouse sink in her green and white apron with a quarter-size strawberry stain on the front. She was the expert, the baker of all things rich and fruity.

Left with no choice, we'd head back into the woods to find those bushes again. We'd disappear for hours. No matter. Our parents didn't care. They never gave us watches or asked us to be back by a certain time. They were enjoying their escape from the clock as well. The women spent their hours cooking and gossiping. The men sat on the opposite side of the kitchen, next to the coffin-size freezer that stood below a cheaply framed print of the Last Supper, listening to a Red Sox game on Pépère's wooden-cased transistor radio. My dad would finally relax. Earlier, he would have been quibbling with my mother.

"How long are you planning to stay?" he'd ask Mom when they were discussing our visit to my grandparents' house.

"I don't know, not long." Mom would respond matter-of-factly. The conversation always ended with Dad agreeing to come, as long as Mom agreed to keep the visit short.

Funny how everything changed as time melted away on the hill.

Looking back, I realize both my parents paid close attention to time. Thirty minutes before we left for mass every Saturday, Dad would start looking at his watch. Regular updates about the time would follow. My parents were usually the first ones to a family event. Sometimes they'd arrive so early, they'd have to stop somewhere to *kill time*, as Dad would say, once they neared their destination. When I was leaving for a semester in London, they brought me to the airport five hours before my flight. The long wait stole the wind from our good-byes.

The beach is another place where time melts away. Having grown up in Massachusetts, my proximity to land's end was a luxury I took for granted. It was only when I moved to Washington D.C. that I realized how much I wanted to be near the ocean. So after ten years I moved back, to be near family and sea.

My relationship with the ocean began at an early age. Since

I was two years old, my family would spend one or two weeks every summer on Cape Cod. The time on the Cape, along with the endless days on my grandparents' hill, formed the centerpiece of my childhood.

The night before our trip, Mom would pack boxes with sheets, towels, sunscreen and bug spray. Dad would organize the trunk of our 1972 Chevy Impala as though it were a puzzle that only he could solve. Then he'd secure bulky suitcases to the roof rack with a rope about a quarter mile long as though expecting to drive across the Himalayas in a thunderstorm.

The bikes came next. I tried to think of what was going through Dad's mind as he attached the bungee cords so securely that not even an Eagle Scout could undo them without the proper tool. What was the worst-case scenario that he was so determined to avoid? In my young mind I pictured bikes flying across the highway, smashing into windshields, people screaming.

Once the bikes were fastened to the back of the car, there was no going back into the trunk. Dad was done for the night.

The next morning, we'd leave at dawn to assure a traffic-free passage over the Sagamore Bridge. Invariably, there was some point along the way when Mom and Dad would bicker over directions, even though we travelled the same route every year. Mom, map in hand, would spout instructions that didn't quite align with Dad's intuition, making him tense up. This exchange always had the same ending: Mom was right, though her smug attitude didn't help matters.

Although Mom was more of a free spirit than Dad, they both enjoyed a hefty portion of order in their lives. Mom was the quintessential list maker. She had lists for everything – holiday meals, birthday gifts, packing essentials. Dad was a routine lover – same restaurants (Marshside and Webster House), same beaches (West Dennis and Nauset), same ice cream flavor (black raspberry).

My parents always took us to the West Dennis Beach because Mom claimed the water was warmer in the Nantucket Sound. Dad would offer me and my brother a quarter if we darted into the water until fully submerged, our eyes burning with salt. I'm only slightly embarrassed to admit this worked every time. When I started doing the same with my kids, I realized it had served as cheap entertainment for my parents.

Nauset Beach, located at the southern end of the National Seashore, was my favorite. We went only once during our weeklong vacation because the water was frigid and we had to pay for parking. My brother and I called it "Big Wave Beach"– I guess because we couldn't remember its real name. The nickname suited it though, and reminded us why we loved it so much. Once comfortably numb, Joey and I would throw ourselves onto the waves and ride them ashore. We ducked under the gigantic ones, lest they swirl us into disorientation. Nothing was more terrifying to a kid.

My parents completely relaxed once they were on the beach, and so did I. When the sun had zapped our last bit of energy, and layers of lotion, sand and salt caked our bodies, we'd return to our cottage to shower, eat and sleep. Then we'd get up to do it all over again.

Life was good.

5

The Beach

"The first time I went to the beach, I was too shy because it was a bunch of white people." -Eugene

"The people were half naked and I thought, 'This is crazy,' because we never saw that before." -Sonia

The WaterFire festival wasn't my bowl of soup, but our next outing with Eugene and Sonia would be splendid. How could it not? We were taking them to my favorite place – the beach. They had never been before, so it promised all the perks of a first-time adventure: excitement, surprise, intrigue.

Although I complained about going to the same place every year when I was a teenager, something about the Cape kept pulling me back, even as an adult. I still felt giddy when the sweet salty air announced my proximity to the ocean –

and again, when the shoreline first came into view. There was nothing like it. I loved the way it ignited all my senses at once, yet never overwhelmed me. I loved the ocean, period. The briny smell of dried seaweed, the rhythmic sound of the slurping surf, the warmth of sand between my toes – all had an unexplainable calming effect on me. I couldn't wait to share this magic with Sonia, Jean Pierre and Eugene.

We couldn't have picked a better beach day. The air was warm and only slightly humid, the sky a bright cerulean blue, which blended into a pale yellow green as it touched the horizon. We arrived at Sonia and Eugene's house just before nine as the sun was taking center stage. Any later and we'd risk the parking lot being full and having to turn back.

Jean Pierre shook our hands when we entered the kitchen, looked us each in the eye. Eugene emerged from his bedroom without acknowledging us. Any excitement he had for the day he kept concealed. Sonia dragged herself sloth-like from her bedroom as if she needed more sleep. We offered Eugene one of Wayne's bathing suits, but he opted to wear shorts. Sonia wore the bathing suit I had bought her, under plaid shorts and a t-shirt.

Forty-five minutes of forced chitchat stood between us and the beach. Without even a first language in common, I struggled to find common ground and to make our friends feel comfortable. I spouted questions as they randomly popped into my head, like I was tossing them scraps of conversation. What kinds of food do you miss? Did you eat pizza in Africa?

They answered politely. Sometimes Eugene had to repeat himself a few times before we understood him.

Then a long silence.

More questions.

Silence again.

I rambled on about our dog and chickens.

More silence while I reloaded my brain with innocuous prompts. Wayne helped a bit, but he was driving. The girls, on the other hand, were useless in this endeavor.

By the time we arrived at the beach, I was relieved and exhausted. I imagined a time in the future when we'd be completely relaxed with one another and chatter would flow easily. Maybe we'd even welcome the occasional dead air space – or at least not have to fight it so hard. I pictured myself at their weddings and playing with their children.

Excitement overtook the awkward silence as we pulled into the mall-size parking lot. Wayne unloaded the beach gear from the back of the Mazda and handed it out. Eugene and Jean Pierre each took a folded canvas chair and flung the long straps over their broad shoulders. Jean Pierre caught Eugene's eye, then glanced down at the chair hanging from his body. "Like guns," he mumbled. He didn't think I heard him, but I did. All of the stories I had read, all of the movies I had watched about child soldiers in Africa flashed through my mind like a disturbing photomontage. I wondered what *these* boys had witnessed. For a moment, the awkward silences seemed insignificant.

For a moment, I had perspective.

I held onto these images as we walked to the edge of the pavement, made our way across the glistening sand not yet heated by the sun. The perfect weather enticed many people to the shore that day, but at this hour there was plenty of room to spread our blanket and set up our chairs. Later it would be packed. Rainbow-colored umbrellas and beach towels would overtake the earth-toned landscape.

The tide was halfway out, but the wind stirred the sea, and the waves taunted us to join them. Jean Pierre and Eugene stared at the blue-green water as if they were calculating the fortitude it would take to accept its invitation. Jean Pierre's eyes were full with determination. Few words were spoken. One thing was certain: If Jean Pierre went in, Eugene would follow.

Jean Pierre didn't waste any time. He yanked off his shirt and, with a running start, plunged into the ocean head first. Eugene gingerly pulled his t-shirt over his head and sauntered to the shore, his eyes fixed on Jean Pierre who was bobbing around like a buoy. Arms above his head, teeth clenched, Eugene waded into the water. The rest of us watched with anticipation as the waves poured over their heads and scooped them up.

The girls and I joined them, but only briefly. We loved the ocean, but didn't approach it with the same hunger. We knew many beach days lay ahead, so we were content to keep Sonia company on dry land and watch the boys lose their inhibition to the sea. I turned my striped beach chair to face Eugene and Jean Pierre like I was adjusting a TV screen. Then I sank into it, stretched my arms and legs for full sun coverage. Wayne reached into our canvas bag for a book, and Sonia sprawled herself on the blanket in front of us. I admired

Wayne and Sonia for doing exactly what they pleased, for not worrying about everyone else.

"Do you want to go in the water, Sonia?"

"No." She scrunched her face and caressed her stomach. "I don't feel good. Maybe next time."

"The boys look like they're having fun." I did a lot of stating of the obvious during our first summer together – anything to prevent the quiet from growing too long.

After almost an hour, the girls and I coaxed Eugene and Jean Pierre out of the water and invited them to walk down the beach to where the ocean met a stream. Jean Pierre ran ahead, then threw himself into multiple back flips like a human Slinky. Perfectly composed, he walked a few steps, then flipped himself three more times as if it were as natural to him as breathing.

"Where did you learn to do that?" I asked. I had never seen anything like it on the beach, and I was certain I never again would.

"In my home country. It's easy," he said. I was unconvinced. A couple more back flips and Jean Pierre was again walking beside us. Moments later, the river came into view and the boys' eyes grew wide.

It looked like a horizontal water slide. In seconds the boys fed themselves to the stream, entertaining the girls with their clumsy attempts to outmaneuver it.

Rachel and Sydney had always lived near the water, and I had insisted they take swimming lessons when they were little. Now they could swim like the stripers cruising along the West Dennis beach. In contrast to Rachel and Sydney's aquatic agility, Eugene and Jean Pierre's style was more haphazard. It was like watching Ginger Rogers and Debbie Reynolds dance with Burt and Ernie. What mattered was that everyone was having fun, and this brought us together. Words weren't necessary anymore. We shared a feeling – the feeling of taking a leap into the unknown and giving in to forces pulling us in an unforeseen direction.

After a few hours everyone's stomach was rumbling, but of course our cooler was empty. It was time to dry off and head home. We'd stop somewhere along the way for something to eat.

We chose a small fast food restaurant on the main drag. Wayne and I waited our turn to order while the others crammed together shoulder to shoulder in a shiny red booth. No one was speaking. Without the shared experience to bring them together, they suddenly had nothing to talk about. Or maybe it was the language barrier or the fact that they were exhausted. Maybe the cavernous silence didn't bother them, but it unraveled me. Indeed, this was a situation that needed fixing. I gestured to Sydney to show the others how to get their drinks from the soda machine, so at least they'd be *doing* something.

Moments later I heard snickering and turned to see what was stirring a commotion. Sydney had demonstrated how to dispense soda from the machine, but the lever became stuck. Diet Coke poured out like a waterfall and flooded the tray below. Sydney struggled to dislodge the lever, but the soda kept flowing. The cumulative giggling gained momentum and erupted into full blown belly-laugher that seemed to burst out from each of them as if it had been held captive deep down inside their souls. Tension released its grip on my shoulders, and I joined the laughter, no faking this time.

Later that evening, sitting on our olive green sofa, Wayne and I reflected on our day with Sonia, Jean Pierre and Eugene.

"What did you and Sonia talk about while we were with the boys?" I said. I plopped my bare feet onto his lap.

"She told me about her aunt who took her and Eugene in when their mother died," he replied. He sipped his beer.

"Really?" I don't know why I was surprised that Sonia had opened up to Wayne. He's a good listener with a genuine interest in other people's stories. And it doesn't hurt that he has sparkling emerald eyes. Sure, sometimes my words bounce off my husband like ping pong balls and disappear into oblivion with all those mismatched socks. But most people find him attentive and easy to talk to.

"Yeah. Their older brothers stayed in Rwanda, but they moved in with their aunt in Zambia. Sonia went to school while Eugene ran the aunt's store."

"Oh, so that's why he couldn't go to school."

"Yeah, I guess." Wayne took another sip of his beer. "I told her not to worry because she would never be alone again."

"What do you mean?" This was a bold statement to blurt to a stranger, I thought, although social norms had never before stopped my husband from expressing himself.

"I told her now that she's met you, she'll never be alone." He rubbed my feet.

"What? How could you make that kind of promise? We just met them! You don't know the future." I could feel the anger contorting my face. My husband didn't respond in kind to my drama. He kept rubbing my feet.

"No, I don't know the future. But I know *you*," he said.

I don't want to give the impression that my husband thought I was a selfless person, or a saint or anything like that. He didn't, I'm pretty sure of that. But he knew that people important to me tended to get lodged in my heart. It had to do with my introverted personality. Introverts tend to form a few lasting relationships rather than have many acquaintances. We may not be the life of the party, but our loyalty to loved ones is puppy strong.

One example of this pattern is the relationship I formed with my "little sister" when I attended Clark University. The Big Brother Big Sister program matched college students with children from the nearby elementary school. The expectation was that the young adults would spend one afternoon each week with their smaller counterparts and commit to maintaining the relationship for one year.

I still remember the day I met six-year-old Melissa. As soon as we knew we were paired together, the skinny girl with crooked bangs took my hand. She won my heart in an instant.

Fast-forward to my wedding day over a decade later. Melissa was a bridesmaid. Without being asked, she posed in our family photographs.

"I'm the only sister you'll ever have," she said as she edged her way into the frame of the picture. I thought nothing of this at the time, but thinking about our relationship now makes me understand what my husband already knew about me.

6

Eugene

"When we went bowling, I didn't know what I was doing, but it was funny. I wish we could go there again." –Eugene

"When we first came here, Robert's sisters wanted me to go to the movies with them. I told them no, I couldn't leave Eugene. They didn't understand. It's because of everything we (Eugene and I) went through before." -Sonia

Later that summer, conversation was flowing more freely between Sonia and me, and her sarcastic humor seeped in on occasion. We e-mailed one another and spoke on the phone. Language and cultural barriers were eroding, allowing our friendship to take root.

We were bonding.

Eugene was a different story. He remained aloof in my family's presence, and it bothered me to think he needed such strong defenses, or maybe he just didn't like us. (I wasn't sure which I thought was worse.) But I was heartened by the subtle ways he was extending himself in our direction. One afternoon, for example, when the girls and I had just come home from visiting my cousin, we noticed a message on our answering machine. We stopped in our tracks when we heard Eugene's unfamiliar telephone voice.

"It's Eugene. I just call to give you hi," he said.

We all looked at each other in delightful disbelief.

"He likes us!" I said. My heart leaped. I felt recognized, appreciated, like a child who had just been patted on the head by a favorite uncle. That was the moment when Eugene secured his place in our hearts. In that moment, I considered it my personal challenge to continue to break down the wall between Eugene and my family. My effort, along with time's patient hand, would dismantle the wall, stone by stone. His message was just the encouragement I needed to keep trying.

To that end, my daughters and I decided to do more activities with Eugene, so one steamy day in August, Rachel, Sydney and I took Eugene and Jean Pierre bowling – something neither of them had done before.

By this time, I was familiar with the drive to Eugene and Sonia's house. It was a couple streets away from Providence's Italian neighborhood, which boasted fancy restaurants, high-end salons and quaint bakeries. Three-story apartments in varying stages of disrepair stood a block away, where Eugene and Sonia lived.

The scent of rain breezed through my window as we pulled into the parking lot of Eugene and Sonia's building. Teenagers loitered across the street. A family sat at a picnic table under a tree growing in a small patch of grass adjacent to the paved lot. We exchanged a friendly nod with them before climbing the two flights of stairs to the apartment.

Eugene let us in without saying a word. After I repeated our plan to make sure he understood, Eugene disappeared into his bedroom, and Sonia came out of her room to greet us. (She had zero desire to join us on our strange adventure.) A few minutes later, Jean Pierre arrived like the sun. With his usual round of handshakes, he greeted us one by one. Eugene returned wearing a steel-blue t-shirt and a blank expression, like a teenager waiting for the morning school bus. I guessed he didn't know how to feel about something he had never done before.

Jean Pierre was the perfect match for Eugene. Friendly and spontaneous, he was game for anything and wore his eagerness like a favorite baseball cap. The boys spent a lot of time together, and I was happy Eugene had made a friend so quickly. I was also grateful to have Jean Pierre around to fill in some of the gaping silences. I saw him as someone who could help break down the barriers between Eugene and my family. But I worried that Eugene thought we favored Jean Pierre because he was easier to talk to.

Jean Pierre's enthusiasm almost convinced me that he understood what we were about to do. But anyone who has gone bowling knows you need to wear socks with bowling shoes; Jean Pierre was wearing flip-flops. I suggested he run back to his house and grab a pair. Eugene, Rachel and Sydney crowded the back seat of the car, and we all waited in silence for Jean Pierre's return. Another long uncomfortable silence. At this point, it felt like we had collected a dumpsterful of them.

Hours instead of minutes seemed to pass before Jean Pierre crossed the street and strutted toward us. He paused when he reached the front passenger door. Then, unexpectedly and without warning, he opened his arms, releasing six tiny sparrows, which flew away as if they suddenly had somewhere important to be. Jean Pierre kept a straight face as if this was something he did every day.

We laughed out loud.

"How did you catch them?" I said.

"They were in my bedroom." He replied as if that was an answer. "We catch small animals in my home country all the time. It's easy."

We kept chuckling as we repeated the scene in our minds, like replaying episodes of our favorite sitcom.

As we pulled out of the parking lot, Jean Pierre gestured toward the young men hanging out in front of his house.

"They're bad," he said.

"They're bad?" I wanted to make sure I heard him correctly. Although Jean Pierre's English was excellent, his accent made him difficult to understand.

"Yes. They sell drugs," he said clearly.

"Right in front of your house?"

"Yeah, they're there all the time," he said.

I felt my mother instinct kick in. "Well, you boys know

not to go near them, right?" Through my rearview I caught Eugene's expression, which registered as goofy teenage smugness. It was the same reaction I would get from my own daughters when they were older, as if to say, "Duh, we're not stupid, Mom."

I decided to leave well enough alone.

This was not the first time I took Eugene to East Providence. We had taken him to the movies and to play miniature golf earlier in the summer. So I had little patience with myself for getting lost. Again. It didn't help that it was now pouring. Or that the conversation was strained. Or that I was getting hungry. With windshield wipers on high speed, I tried to conjure up a mental map to discern our location, but I was distracted by the dark thoughts zipping around my head: *This sucks. I'm miserable, and they're miserable.*

As we finally pulled into the parking lot of the bowling alley, I forced myself to breathe. My goal was to show Eugene a good time, so I pasted an expression on my face that I hoped read "yay." I wondered why I needed to go to superhero lengths to keep everyone smiling. Why couldn't I just relax and enjoy myself? I wondered if I was doomed to be this way for all eternity.

When we entered the cadet-gray building, I was surprised to find a small bright room – a stark contrast to the place where I had bowled as a child. This place had a cheerful feel to it. The one near my house growing up had five times as many lanes and looked like a dark subway station. At least that's how it lived in my memory.

After a couple tries, and with minimal instruction, Eugene

and Jean Pierre looked like pros. To my daughters' amazement, Eugene won the first game, and Jean Pierre was a close second. Beginner's luck, we thought.

Soon my kids complained of being hungry. I wished I had planned the day better so I wouldn't feel compelled to pay unreasonable prices for food that was mediocre at best. One game didn't feel long enough to justify the effort to get there, so another was in order. I felt a twinge of discomfort as I tallied the cost of our brief outing.

But luck was with all of us that day. As we were finishing our second game, the power went out. The owner explained that, because the credit card machine wasn't working, everything was "on the house." He gave out t-shirts with black and white cartoons on the front, and fabric markers to fill them in. We weren't able to finish our second game, but Eugene and Jean Pierre colored in every detail outlined on the front of their new shirts.

We left with t-shirts and full stomachs, and I was satisfied with the time we had spent together. Eugene wore his t-shirt often, and I smiled every time I saw him in it.

That summer was filled with many firsts for Eugene and Sonia, including their first visit to our home one evening in mid-July.

My anxieties came out of the closet just in time. I imagined what they might think: *Those privileged white people have it so easy.* Don't get me wrong – we had a modest home by most people's standards. Built in the fifties, it had neither historic charm nor modern amenities. Three dorm-size bedrooms and one full bath accommodated the four of us. It had no finished basement, eat-in kitchen, or family room. Our living room, furnished with an old piano and rummage sale bookshelves, was cozy-plain. Standing in the middle of it, an old friend described me as a minimalist, if that says anything. Still, as I mentally prepared myself for their visit, I couldn't help but fear they'd feel uncomfortable in my home, decide they didn't like us.

I went through my usual stress-reducing cleaning regimen, prepared vegetarian lasagna in advance, and changed out of my comfy sweatpants. A cemented smile would hide any signs of worry.

We brought them out to our coop and introduced them to our six hens. I imagined they thought it strange how we treated the birds like pets rather than prospective meals. But they listened attentively as we chatted on and on about their unique quirks and personalities.

When the lasagna was heated, we gathered around the table in our cramped dining room. It was suitable for our non-entertaining family of four, but felt suddenly inadequate when guests were in our midst. Besides the table, an Amish desk (a family heirloom) and a jumbo dog crate, draped with a checkered tablecloth, devoured the space.

"Why don't we say grace?" Wayne blurted before anyone had a chance to dig in. Disapproval pursed Sydney's lips. Rachel giggled. Wayne said grace twice a year: Thanksgiving and Easter. This was neither. He did, however, routinely surprise us with the words that sailed out of his mouth. When this happened in front of other people, the girls and I clamped our mouths shut and gulped our laughter – as if we were all in on a private joke.

After Wayne said grace, I scooped hefty portions of lasagna onto plates, and we got right down to the business of eating. Eugene and Sonia looked guarded, like they were afraid to make a wrong move. I steadied my nerves and hoped my positive energy would put them at ease. We asked a lot of questions, and they answered as best they could. Encouraging them to eat more, I suddenly felt like Mémère. There was nothing more satisfying to her than cooking for someone with a healthy appetite.

After every meal, Mémère would immediately sweep away the dirty dishes – another quirk handed down from Mémère to Mom to me. That one didn't skip a generation, as some do.

As if a victim of kooky genetics, I wasted no time getting the dirty dishes off the table. I gave the girls my *please don't make me ask you to help* look and they sprang into action. Of course, they were eager to get on with dessert. Another family trait. We didn't waste time getting to dessert. There was no time-out portion of the meal, no chance to let your stomach settle. If you didn't pace yourself during the main course, you'd suffer.

As I doled heaping scoops of gooey pecan pie onto plates, Sonia told me something about herself that made me skeptical we could ever be close: She didn't like sweets.

After dinner, Rachel and Sydney challenged Eugene to a game of foosball in the garage, and he accepted. Eugene lasered his focus and battled the plastic soccer players as if there was something on the line besides his ego.

"It's two to three, now," I said looking on.

"Four!" Eugene corrected in a booming voice I hadn't heard before.

Our ability to devote uninterrupted hours to building a relationship with Eugene came to a halt at the end of July when he got a job. The employment coordinator at the International Institute helped him get a dishwashing position at a plush hotel on Goat Island overlooking Newport Harbor. The Institute provided the hotel with a steady stream of hard working, motivated employees; the hotel managers committed to training refugees with diverse backgrounds and varying English proficiencies. It was a win–win.

Although Eugene was fortunate to be hired so quickly, his job had one major drawback: It was an hour and a half away by public transportation. Eugene had to take a bus downtown and then another to Newport. His days were suddenly gobbled up by his job and commute.

Eugene never complained about his situation, and I'm sure the steady paycheck brought him relief. He and Sonia had both been concerned about how they'd pay their bills if they weren't hired by the time their financial support was up. I told them they needn't worry because the employment coordinator at the Institute assured me they'd be taken care of until they found jobs, but my words didn't appease them.

I knew Eugene had aspirations beyond his dishwashing job. He wanted an education, a good job, and a better life for himself. Regardless of his next step, I knew he'd benefit from an ESL (English as a Second Language) class. Since he seemed willing to do anything I suggested, I decided to find him one. His inability to pay, his work schedule, and the fact that many classes were already into their summer session narrowed the options. Eventually I found a class near the International Institute, though there was a fee.

After several e-mails and phone calls, I managed to get the fee waived. Then there was the registration. Students had to sign up in person, but not at the time the course was offered, so Eugene would have to miss a day of work early on in his employment. I repeatedly explained the situation to the woman in charge, and eventually convinced her to make another exception for Eugene. But he'd have to arrive early on the first day of class. I cleared my schedule and told Eugene the plan. I picked him up and brought him to the class at the designated time, but the woman wasn't there, and she hadn't told anyone about our situation. Driving Eugene home, I thought out loud about how this miscommunication could've happened, and I apologized to Eugene as if it were my fault.

After another round of phone calls and e-mails, we had a new game plan to get him registered.

A couple weeks after he started class, I called to see how it was going.

"I quit." Eugene did not sound happy.

"What happened?" I could feel my blood pressure rise. *After all that and you just quit?*

"The teacher spoke in Spanish the whole time. I didn't understand," he answered in a clipped voice that forbade any questions. I worried that Eugene might decide I was an idiot for making him leap through thirty hoops to listen to a Spanish-speaking instructor teach him how to speak English. Even in the best case scenario, I couldn't have been earning trust points with him.

7

——

Moses Brown School

"I was very shy because I never had a boyfriend before. Robert was very serious about me, but I wasn't sure if I was ready for a relationship." -Sonia

Most of my hours away from Eugene and Sonia were spent less than three miles from their apartment, but I may as well have been on a different planet. I taught in the posh east side neighborhood of Providence at an independent Quaker school.

I started working at Moses Brown in the fall of 1998, one month after discovering I was pregnant with Sydney. Wayne and I had moved from Maryland to be closer to my family in Massachusetts, and the opportunity to teach at an independent school with a daycare for faculty children was more than I had hoped for.

My memory of the day I interviewed remains untarnished while others seem to gather dust as I forge my way through middle age. The flight from Baltimore lasted just over an hour. I made the round trip in a single day, toting only a small carry-on that fit beneath the seat in front of me with loads of room to spare. I always imagined that people who travelled without luggage were CEOs of major corporations or famous actors. That I suddenly found myself among them made me feel mysterious and important at the same time.

The math department head knew I was choosing a school for Rachel as well as myself. So she arranged tours of the lower school, woodshop and art studio, as well as the upper school. In one of the lower-school classrooms, a woman, six-tyish, was playing a piano while five focused first-graders, arranged in a semi-circle, sang "Puff the Magic Dragon." The music teacher didn't seem even slightly jaded by her years spent with this lively population. Instead, she exuded kindness, joy and purpose like she was Mrs. Clause, Mother Goose and Mary Poppins all wrapped into one. She helped the children along, nodding in affirmation while joining them in song. Her command and direction were apparent to adult eyes only, as the children, captivated by her passion, released a sweet melody for the sheer pleasure of it. It was one of those moments when everything seemed clear: This was the school I wanted my children to attend.

The campus, with its traditional brick buildings and manicured grounds, appeared aloof and pretentious to passersby.

The most prominent building, the one visible from the main street, lorded over the east side of Providence, bowing only to its prestigious neighbor, Brown University. A black wrought-iron gate wrapped itself around the property, as if protecting it from intruders. Just outside the gate, Lexuses, BMWs and Infinity SUVs parked along the curb.

I've always been proud of the fact that I taught at Moses Brown. And why wouldn't I be? It was one of the most highly regarded schools in Rhode Island, and the student body consisted of entrepreneurs, musicians, artists and budding scientists who'd continue their education at Harvard, Brown, Tufts and MIT. Moses Brown teachers developed their own curricula and had access to a variety of resources for their classrooms and professional development.

Why, then, was I not proud to admit that my daughters attended MB? My first reaction when I told someone where my daughters went to school was, "It's only because I teach there and get a huge discount. I couldn't afford the tuition otherwise." I resisted being clumped with the average tuition-paying Moses Brown parent because I didn't want people to think I had more money than I did. People are funny about money. It can divide them, put them on separate planes.

Although many of the students shared the same privileged background, their personalities and interests were as varied as the colors in my teenage daughter's nail polish collection. That was one of the many reasons I loved teaching there.

But I often dreaded the start of a new school year. The first autumn after meeting Eugene and Sonia was no exception.

If anything, I started the mourning process earlier – bidding an emotional farewell to stretches of unstructured time where I was as likely to ride my bike all day as spend four hours glue-gunning seashells together in a clumsy attempt to imitate a wreath I had seen in an oceanside gift shop. The summer flew by too quickly, as always. My days would now be structured – from the moment I got up to the time I went to bed. It would take creative time management to keep up my exercise routine. Any extra time I had at the end of the day, once classes were planned, papers graded and dinner cleared, would be spent curled up on the sofa in my sweats watching a recorded soap opera or new episode of *Finding Bigfoot*.

At the beginning of each school year, I promised myself I'd make time to run and paint. These daily summer activities seemed essential to my happiness, maybe even my sanity. Still, I realized this was an empty promise because the truth was that I'd allow my time to be consumed by other commitments. Once the school year started, I'd feel like I was trapped on a fast-moving treadmill, until the next vacation or long weekend crept into my peripheral vision. This truth gave me a sick feeling in the pit of my stomach.

On the other hand, I loved the opportunity to start anew each year. There was something oddly exciting about filling in my new plan book and school calendar for the first time. I'd write in the names of my classes as neatly as I could, and wonder for a moment if it would look better in color. I'd vacuum my book bag, sharpen pencils and place them in the pencil holder in the third pocket on the front of the bag with the intention of keeping them in their rightful place all year. These rituals quelled my anxiety.

I imagine this is what the packing routine did for my parents every summer – gave them the illusion of control over their worries – until the tide could wash them away once they were on the safe side of the Sagamore Bridge. Maybe the need for control was a family trait, something I would pass on to my children, *bless their hearts,* as my mother-in-law would say.

Fortunately, our teaching schedule allowed us to ease back into our routine. The first week back, we had two days of meetings followed by a long weekend, then four days of classes.

This first day for teachers began with silent worship at the Quaker Meeting House, located on the edge of campus. Quakers believe that God can speak through anyone, and this unprogrammed meeting provided an opportunity for that to happen. If someone felt moved to speak, he was encouraged to break the silence with his message.

During the academic year, the entire upper school gathered weekly for a thirty-minute meeting for worship. Although it wasn't uncommon for the half hour to pass without anyone speaking, more often the silence was broken by voices of teachers and students sharing heartfelt messages. Of course, there were times when well-meaning students sounded as if they were free-associating as one unedited thought led to another. In those cases, it was difficult to decipher the underlying nugget of wisdom one should take away. Except for the fear that my empty stomach would rumble in the silence, I looked forward to sitting quietly with colleagues and students.

We'd tell students that when no one was speaking, they should worship silently or center themselves, though I was never sure what that meant – centering oneself. I usually let my mind wander aimlessly, and I was surprised by the memories and ideas that revealed themselves in the stillness.

One time my mind drifted to my first pair of jeans (Toughskins). Mom made my clothes when I was young. She sewed my shirts and elastic-waist pants from the same fabric, a sturdy cotton with a colorful print. One day when I was in seventh grade, she brought me to the Auburn Mall to pick out my first pair of jeans. You would've thought she had bought me the Eiffel Tower, I was so excited! I hadn't thought about those jeans in years, but there they were in my mind's eye during a Quaker meeting – until I suddenly remembered a meeting I had during lunch, then wondered if I had brought enough warm clothes for my run that afternoon. That was my centering.

A recurring theme popped up in messages from students who had experienced loss or tragedy: Be present. When I heard this I thought, yes – I want to be present. But I wasn't sure *how* to be present. I knew when I *was* present, but it was never by intention. I felt most in the moment when the unexpected happened, when I was caught off guard and there was no time to censor my thoughts or assess how anxious I should be. I knew I had felt completely in the moment in the woods behind my grandparents' house. But then again, the unexpected could happen at any moment there. Like the time a bull freed itself from Pépère's jury-rigged pen and stumbled across my cousin and me picking berries. My memory insists the bull chased us, but that may be one of those childhood memory distortions induced by terror.

The unexpected also occurred frequently on the Cape. I'm not sure if it had more to do with the place or my frame of mind when I was there. Or both. The sea was ever-changing and unpredictable. And the juxtaposition of water and land created an abundance of nooks and crannies just waiting to be discovered. Whatever it was about that place that corrected my perspective, I wished I could stuff it in my purse and carry it everywhere.

This Quaker meeting consisting of all faculty members was not much different from the ones with students. One colleague spoke of their son, a recent MB graduate, and what the school had meant to him. Another shared words of support for a teacher whose father had recently died. I gulped my tears more than once, and forced myself to think of something less serious until the meeting ended with the shaking of hands.

Friendly chatter filled the sanctuary as people continued to catch up with one another. We moseyed to the opposite side of campus where we again quieted ourselves, so key people from different departments could bombard us with details of campus improvements, student enrollment and future plans. By this time I was ready for a nap.

Eventually my mind jerked back to reality when someone said "lunch." It would be the only leisurely lunch we'd have all year. The hour almost seemed too long, but I reminded myself of the twenty-five minute lunches I'd soon have, and I was suddenly grateful.

My day ended with a meeting of upper school teachers. The head of upper school, academic dean, and dean of students hustled through start-of-the-year logistics. This particular first day back was ordinary so far, and I again found my mind drifting back to the long summer days of running, biking and painting.

I was a textbook introvert. Talking to people sapped my energy; solitude restored it. This explains why I was a better human being during the summer and why these meetings marked a difficult transition for me.

My mind drifted toward images of the serene Cape Cod bay, the sweet smell of the marsh, the hustle and bustle of Provincetown. I yanked myself back to present when I realized the head of upper school was describing a new student from Africa, though I didn't catch what part. Her name was Chantal. She had arrived in the United States three years ago as a refugee. The head of upper school explained that Chantal was doing so well at a public school in Providence that our school decided to "take a chance on her" and accept her as a junior.

Although Africa was an expansive continent, I couldn't help but wonder if this girl was from Rwanda as were Sonia and Eugene. It seemed too unlikely to consider for more than a passing moment.

A couple weeks later I visited Sonia on my way home from

school. She still hadn't found a job and was growing impatient.

"Hi Chris," she said without excitement when she opened the door. I could see a man behind her. Annet's brother, Robert, was sitting at the kitchen table, dressed in khaki pants and a maroon button-down shirt. If Sonia hadn't told me he was twenty-three, I would've guessed he was older. His masculine build and confident air read as maturity. Robert had been stopping by to see Sonia every day after work. He looked comfortable in her home. Sonia paid little attention to him, and I wondered if his presence annoyed her. She clearly didn't carry the same cross I did – of having to fake a cheerful mood.

I later learned that Sonia and Robert had a lot in common. Also from Rwanda and born into a large family, Robert understood the devastation and hardship Sonia had endured – and the challenges of piecing together a new life in a strange land. Robert and his older brothers had come to the U.S. as refugees five years earlier. Since then, his two sisters had joined them.

Robert was taking classes at the local community college while working at a nursing home. He seemed happy to help Sonia navigate her educational path, and I was grateful she had someone with a similar background to guide her. Sonia didn't have a high school degree and was too old to attend public school. The good news was that she could attend the local community college without taking the GED (General Educational Development) test. The college had the resources to help emigrants pursue their education, regardless of their background.

Robert had found Sonia, Eugene and Emmanuel a nicer apartment for approximately the same rent, and had made arrangements for them to move at the end of the month. Sonia was anxious to leave her dingy apartment. She especially hated the cramped living room.

We talked about the details of the move because Wayne and I were planning to help. I wasn't sure how Robert was planning to move the furniture since he didn't have a truck. He kept trying to explain his plan, but there was one word I didn't understand because of his accent. It sounded like "you hole." After making him repeat the word numerous times, it was as if someone turned a light on in my head: Robert was saying "U-Haul."

"Oh!" I said when it finally registered, "That's a great idea."

At some point in the conversation, I mentioned my job.

"Where do you teach?" Robert asked.

"At Moses Brown." I assumed that meant nothing to him.

"You teach at Moses Brown?" Robert sounded surprised and strangely interested.

"Yes."

"My sister goes there," Robert said, his voice dripping with pride. "Her name is Chantal."

8

Practical Matters

"I was excited about going to school because I was planning my future." -Eugene

I scanned my flooded e-mail inbox for messages requiring immediate attention. Later I'd go through them with more scrutiny, deleting the junk. That's what I promised myself on this early October morning.

E-mails are a gift to introverts. We can work with people without actually working *with* people. Also, introverts take longer to process information, and e-mail allows us time to think before we respond to another's request – to properly assemble our words so we don't sound stupid.

On the other hand, hours are flushed away each week clicking on and deleting the garbage. In many cases, too much time is wasted responding to messages that would never have demanded our attention if e-mail didn't exist. I'm convinced of this.

My eyes lingered on a message from Taylor Rubins. Subject: Eugene. Taylor was the educational coordinator at the International Institute. She told me that Eugene was finally enrolled as a sophomore at Riverdell High School, one of Providence's nine public high schools, with just under a thousand students. It was, according to several sources, one of the lowest ranking public schools in the state. The positive tone of the e-mail implied a cause for celebration.

I was skeptical.

How was he going to succeed with a less than stellar grasp of the English language? How was he going to catch up after missing the first weeks of school? What support system did they have for students like Eugene? I needed someone, *anyone*, to convince me that everything was going to work out. I'm not a dramatic person, but I am up against a worry gene I inherited squarely from my mother.

I e-mailed my concerns to the educational coordinator and left several phone messages. No response. I guessed she had more important things to do than appease a worrywart like me.

I was also obsessing over Eugene and Sonia's financial situation. Sonia had recently started working at the same hotel as Eugene, but he was working only weekends now that he was a student. Sonia's pay would have to cover the bulk of their expenses. I wondered how they'd get by. I wondered if Eugene would have time to get his homework done on the weekends. Maybe I was being a nervous Nelly. Or maybe I was beginning to care deeply about my young friends.

In the following weeks, phone calls and e-mails swallowed my free periods at school. My goals, I thought, were simple: to get Eugene a tutor and to help him procure the food stamps and free lunches he was entitled to. Once I started on this mission, I felt like I was swimming upstream with the herring on Cape Cod. Everyone I spoke to relayed different information. "You need to contact *this* person," is something I grew tired of hearing. But *this person* never picked up the phone, responded to e-mails or returned phone calls.

The blather pouring out of my receiver made me want to scream. Why was this so difficult? I thought of those who didn't have English-speaking friends to make phone calls on their behalf and this fueled my anger. And I'm not an angry person. I rarely lose my temper with anyone besides my immediate family members. But that's bound to happen with people you communicate with on a level of honesty that borders on insensitivity.

Whenever I thought I had resolved the lunch situation, I'd later discover I was wrong. Each time I saw Eugene, I'd say, "Are you getting your lunches now? You should be getting them."

"No," he'd reply. I'd stare at him, brows furrowing. "But it's all right." He always said that, like he didn't want to upset me. I guess I couldn't hide my fury when I learned the boy was still going hungry during the day.

A social worker informed me that Eugene had missed an interview required for him to get food stamps. (I was certain he wasn't aware of this.) She said Eugene would get another letter informing him of his new interview date. He'd have to leave school early and Wayne would have to drive him to his appointment.

Sonia and Eugene bumped into some of the same challenges when it was time to move. Simple tasks such as disconnecting their utilities and reconnecting them in their new apartment were difficult without a solid grasp of English, or an understanding of what needed to be done. If Sonia was present, she could grant me permission to speak on her behalf, so during one of my free periods I rushed to her house to make the necessary calls and help her through some of the decisions she needed to make.

Making phone calls on Eugene and Sonia's behalf was complicated by the fact that Rwandan names are different from American names. Rwandans don't actually have family names. Instead, when they're born, the father chooses a Kinyarwanda name for the first name and a simpler, usually Christian, name for the last name. It is usually French, but sometimes English. However, when they come to the United States, it is their second name that is most appropriate to use as their first name. For example, Eugene's African name was Nyillingondo Eugene, but he went by Eugene Nyillingondo in the U.S.

Sonia's name was more complicated because she had a middle name, Umotonie. When she arrived, her social worker mistakenly recorded Umotonie as her first name. Her African name was Mutamuliza Umotonie Sonia, and the American name she used was Sonia Umotonie Mutamuliza, but her *official* American name was Umotonie Sonia Mutamuliza.

Lucky for me, Wayne made more than his share of phone calls when it came to Sonia and Eugene. I hated calling people. Well, maybe hate is too strong a word, but my feelings were within spitting distance of hate. In fact, it's one of the many tasks I unwittingly assigned to my husband when we married. I imagine it's this way with many couples: tasks are divided according to who is best suited to complete them. I, for one, was the only member of our household who could wrap a present without the package looking like it was done blindfolded with one hand tied to a railing.

It took a couple months for Eugene to get his food stamps, and he went several weeks without eating lunch at school. He also needed a tutor. Although the International Institute had a list of volunteer tutors, I decided to tap into the resources at my immediate disposal: my students.

My classroom was tucked away in the corner on the second floor of one of the main academic buildings on campus. The room held four large tables and a small desk that organized my grade book, lesson plans, and other teaching materials. Sticky notes decorated its surface, serving as visual cues to what I imagined other people kept in their memory. On this day, there were only a few notes. One stood out because it was written in bold black marker: tutors for Eugene.

As I checked my e-mail and looked over lesson plans, my advisees trickled in. First was Raymond, a ninth-grade boy with a round nose. He was usually the first one to show up in the morning, and I suspected it was because my classroom

was where he felt most comfortable – not because he nec-
essarily liked me. I say this because he had that awkward *I
don't know what to do with myself* look. I recognized this look
on many ninth graders at the beginning of the school year.
You could see them standing for long minutes at their lock-
ers, pretending to busy themselves with something important, like checking their cell phones.

A few more advisees came in. I tried to engage them by
asking about their classes, after-school activities, or favorite
TV shows. The pressure to keep up the conversation vanished
when Katie burst in. Katie was always happy, even when she
was complaining. She had a way of centering the attention
onto herself without being overly dramatic or annoying.

"Jess is stuck in traffic. She texted me," Katie said. She
plopped her backpack on the floor and sank into a chair next
to her friend, Casey.

"Thanks," I said. "How are you doing?" That's all I needed
to say to get her started on a blow by blow of her previous
afternoon.

"I'm so tired!" She threw her arms and head onto the table
and let out an audible breath. "Do you want to hear what I
did last night?" She picked her head up, and I nodded.

"Well, first I had a two-hour soccer practice. Then I had
batting practice with my coach for an hour and a half. I had
an SAT class after that. Then I had to shower, eat dinner and
do my homework."

"But today should be better?" I knew the answer. Katie's
life was completely structured, but by her choice. She was
highly ambitious and would have it no other way. I listened

as sympathetically as I could, and I really didn't mind most of the time. Her bubbly personality made up for the whiney words.

After Katie vented, I quickly read aloud the daily bulletin, which highlighted important student information. Seconds before I dismissed the group, Jess popped in looking exhausted already, her long hair pulled back in a messy ponytail.

"I'm here."

"Thanks, have a great day."

Five minutes later my AP Calculus students wandered in. Teenagers are not morning people. The advantage to our confusing rotating schedule was that I saw students from each course at different times. Later in the day, this would've been a much livelier group. What I loved about teenagers – when they were awake – was how they behaved like caricatures of their later adult selves. They were witty and funny and had big personalities. Instead of feeding off their energy as I would if it were later in the day, I felt it was *my* job to get *them* going on this gray mid-October morning.

Slow as snails, they shed their sleepiness and came to life. They took notes, asked questions and worked together on problems I assigned. When class was over, students packed their notebooks and supplies into their already full backpacks. A positive energy filled the room. Students chatted with me and amongst themselves as they prepared to transition to their next class. I was pleased with myself for suddenly remembering the sticky note on my desk, and I asked one student to stay after class. I had done my research beforehand: I'd ask Kyle.

Like Eugene, Kyle had a small frame. His sharp features and compelling eyes made him look wiser than his teenage years. He was a friendly outgoing boy with a can-do attitude that was almost as remarkable as his capacity for caring. He was the president of the student senate and well-suited for the position. Kyle didn't have to be persuaded to help Eugene; he was eager. I told him that I also planned to ask Dan, another student of mine. Little did I know that Kyle and Dan were good friends, making them a perfect match. Although both boys were dedicated, Dan had transportation issues and a busy sports schedule, so Kyle became Eugene's main source of help that school year.

I left my classroom satisfied with the positive response from Kyle and Dan, and eager to set the plan in motion. It would have to wait though, because right now the Learning Center awaited me. Located across campus, the Learning Center was a place where students could get academic help after school. Teachers rotated at the beginning of each athletic season, and I was one of the two math teachers who worked there in the fall. My commitment in the winter was to the debate team, and I was happy that, for now, my afternoon obligation didn't require preparation. In other words, I just showed up and helped.

I dropped my backpack onto a small table in one of the cubicles and pulled out a pile of calculus tests, a green fine-point Sharpie and my reading glasses. While grading, I kept an eye out for students seeking math help.

None of my own students would show up today. The flow of traffic coincided with assessments, and they had recently taken a test. If anyone came, it would be from someone else's class. And a few did show up. One was my new friend, Chantal.

After the talk with Robert at Sonia's apartment, I introduced myself to Chantal at school. She was on the field hockey team and made friends quickly. Chantal had a genial mouth and sparkling eyes that matched her outgoing personality. You couldn't help but like the girl. She had developed close relationships with several of my students. One time, she came into my calculus class and sat at a table beside the door, straight-faced as if she belonged there. Smiles crept onto my students' faces as they filed in and saw the misplaced student sitting by the door. Seconds before class, Chantal popped up, waved good-bye and vanished in one fluid motion.

I couldn't stop thinking about her – how she joined disparate parts of my life. Immersed in the same school culture, Chantal and I automatically had a lot in common. Strangely, she was more familiar with a part of my life than Eugene and Sonia ever would be. This realization both unsettled and intrigued me.

Chantal had come to the Learning Center to get help with her math homework, and I invited her to sit next to me. She showed me the problems that challenged her, and I explained how to solve them. She was quick to tell me not to give her *too* much help, as she wanted to do the work on her own.

"I don't want anyone to take pity on me," she said.

And I didn't.

9

Autumn Into Winter

"When I started working, Robert would come to Newport to pick me up. Some days I would leave before he got there. He was very nice to me and I liked him, but I was a little scared." -Sonia

Wayne, Robert, Jean Pierre and I helped Eugene and Sonia move on Halloween night. I had anticipated hordes of disguised children roaming the suburbs in groups small and large. The only other time I had been in a city on Halloween night was when I went to Georgetown with my roommate, she as a witch and I as a Christmas tree. We rode the metro into Washington, D.C. and giggled at how silly we looked. In Georgetown we blended right in with the crowd of twenty-somethings masquerading as superheroes, monsters and inanimate objects. I was disappointed that my hand-made blinking costume wasn't all that original.

Only a few trick-or-treaters paraded around Eugene and Sonia's neighborhood. There was no hoopla, just a few dedicated parents passing down the strange tradition to their children. I wondered what Sonia and Eugene thought of this American ritual which suddenly seemed ludicrous when I explained it out loud: costumed children going up to strangers' houses, asking for a treat and threatening to play a trick on the stranger if they didn't get one. I wished I remembered how this custom had originated. Without its historical context, it just sounded wacky – and in a disturbing kind of way.

It was an unusually mild fall evening, ideal for trick or treating – the kind I had always hoped for when I was a kid, so I wouldn't have to wear a coat over the costume I'd been looking forward to wearing for weeks.

I felt in need of a shower after I climbed the dark staircase to Eugene and Sonia's apartment a second time. Half-filled boxes of dishes and pans, garbage bags stuffed with linens, and an assortment of small appliances welcomed us at the top. Sonia let the boys and me do the bulk of the heavy work. Her small frame wasn't suited for such labor, and she busied herself packing the remaining items in her apartment. I tried not to be annoyed that they hadn't finished packing. It's an unspoken rule of etiquette, isn't it, that boxes will be packed before friends arrive to help move them? Perhaps the rule isn't universal.

When both vehicles were loaded, Robert sat in the driver's seat of the U-Haul, and the boys got into the back seat of our Mazda. Night had fallen, but I could see Robert gesture to

Sonia to join him in the van. She acknowledged his invitation with a nod. Then she got into *our* car.

How did Sonia feel toward Robert? He held up his intentions like a picket sign, but her body language was inconsistent. Mysterious. Robert didn't seem deterred. Or surprised.

"Eugene, why don't you go with Robert," I said. It made no sense for Robert to travel alone while we stuffed ourselves in my car like socks in a drawer.

I wondered what Robert thought of Sonia's decision to ride with us.

As we drove to their new home, Wayne grilled Jean Pierre, trying to uncover his story. The oldest of seven, he lived with his siblings and mother, all of whom had come to the United States as refugees. He was a year away from his high-school graduation.

"What do you want to do after you graduate?" Wayne asked.

"Go to college."

"What will you study?"

"I'll get my pilot's license."

"You want to be a pilot?"

"Maybe."

We drove through a dark, run-down neighborhood that seemed devoid of human life – just a few abandoned buildings, a car repair shop that looked more like a junkyard, and a dog walking purposefully down the street.

"You can let me out here," Jean Pierre said. Wayne looked at me, perplexed. I shrugged.

"I have to go to my karate lesson." I followed his gaze

79

toward a lonely lit-up building. Through the windows we saw several young men in karate uniforms, waiting for instruction. Wayne pulled the car over and Jean Pierre jumped out.

"Thank you," he said.

"Do you have a ride home?"

"Yes." He ran off in the direction of the karate studio. And that was that. As we pulled away, we laughed.

We parked the vehicles in the small lot behind the new apartment and entered through the back door, which led to the kitchen. A hallway, with bedrooms off of it, connected the kitchen to the living room in the front of the building. Robert's much older sister, Annet, was cleaning appliances and unpacking kitchen boxes. I introduced myself and told her of my connection to Chantal. As I spoke, she held my hand between hers, and her eyes widened with pleasure. I hoped I'd see her again.

As autumn morphed into winter and days grew shorter, I felt the force of nature pushing me indoors. If I had my way, I'd hibernate through March and come out only once the earth had thawed and plants were springing back to life. And I'd be content in my isolation. I'd read, paint, write – do all my favorite solitary activities until I just had to emerge from my den with the coming of spring, after about five months.

But, alas, life's demands do not slow to nature's pace during the bleak months of winter. I hurried to prepare for my favorite holiday in time to enjoy the season without stress.

That was a lofty goal, I knew, but one I held myself to every year.

I love Christmas. I love the decorations, the carols, the eggnog – every bit of it, but I hate shopping. There is nothing I'd rather do less than leave my warm house in the winter to visit a bustling mall. The fluorescent lights, neon signs and eager shoppers overwhelm me, make me grouchy – especially if I don't take adequate snack breaks. Instead, I scurry around looking for bargains in October when the stores are empty. I finish my shopping online – in my pajamas drinking tea. This works for me.

I wanted to do something special with Sonia and Eugene this Christmas season. About forty minutes from our house was a monastery called The National Shrine of Our Lady of La Salette. Each year, over 500,000 lights decorated the ten acres of grounds, and over 250,000 visitors perused the Stations of the Cross, relics of saints, and nativity displays. While some came to light candles, pray or enjoy the spiritual celebration, others made it a family outing. There was, after all, a hayride, a carousel, and a donkey named Clopper. We thought this would be something that would put us all in the holiday spirit, and we were sure Eugene and Sonia had never seen anything like it.

Christmas music and eggnog beforehand prepped my mood as I convinced myself this would be fun, even if it meant leaving the warmth of my electric blanket. Two layers of socks, a chunky knit fisherman's sweater and an ugly red and brown trapper hat shielded me from the cold. I was determined not to let the nipping air get the best of me.

A dispassionate pair of teenagers greeted us at Eugene and Sonia's apartment. Like a camp counselor, I saw it as my responsibility to orchestrate the fun. I was resentful that my family didn't have the same hang-ups I did, otherwise they might have been more helpful in these situations. Of course, Sonia and Eugene had no idea where we were going as much as we tried to explain to them. But once they saw the brilliant colors against the dark sky, they would be in awe. At least that's what I kept telling myself on the tediously silent drive, broken up only by my sporadic questions.

"We're almost there," I said as soon as I saw a hint of light flickering in the distance. As the lights came fuller into view, I focused all my attention on their reaction. If they were at all impressed, they kept their expressions under stern restraint.

We walked past a large reflecting pool surrounded by elaborate illuminated displays, a smaller pool dotted with multicolored water fountains and a life-size nativity all aglow. Lights dangled from trees above our heads, immersing us in the translucent spectacle. It was magical.

I found myself walking briskly, but I wasn't sure if it was because I was anxious or cold. Probably both. I slowed when I reached the Stations of the Cross and pretended to read the descriptions. Eugene was shivering like I had never seen anyone shiver before: teeth chattering, lips quivering, body trembling. He looked like he could use a hot toddy.

This was not going the way I had hoped.

We walked a bit more before retreating indoors to get hot chocolate. (They didn't sell hot toddies.) When we were ready, we finished our tour and headed back to the car.

It was a quick visit but everyone was hungry and cold (except me, because I was wearing my ugly hat and two pairs of socks). We drove to Olive Garden for dinner. If they hated the light display, at least they'd go home with full stomachs.

We lucked into an instantly available table for six – no wait. As I looked around, I saw the restaurant through a new lens, the way I imagined Eugene and Sonia saw it. Although Olive Garden was a casual family restaurant, it suddenly seemed too fancy. With all its perfect lighting, shiny wooden bar and formally dressed waiters, it felt like the wrong choice. Sonia and Eugene did not look happy. Did they think we were rich people who could afford to eat anywhere we wanted? And if they did, would it matter to them? Did they feel uncomfortable because we were paying for their meal?

Wayne and the girls thought nothing of the situation. Rachel and Sydney discussed what meal they'd split – pasta and a side salad – and Wayne ordered himself a Harpoon IPA and mozzarella sticks to share. I read Eugene and Sonia's deadpan expressions as misery. I only wanted them to feel at ease with us. From that standpoint, this evening was a colossal failure.

"They're usually better than this," Wayne said. He was eating a mozzarella stick. "They're not cooked all the way through." I flashed a look at Rachel that said *Oh, God, no, please don't let my husband embarrass us by sending them back.* (I have a bad habit of asking God for stupid favors.) When the waiter came, I told him the food was delicious before Wayne had a chance to say otherwise. Then I took a deep breath and exhaled my anxiety, prepared to enjoy my food. We ate in relative silence. Eugene and Sonia said the food was good, but they were probably just being polite.

Christmas was different. Eugene and Sonia joined us in the evening and we had a simple meal, exchanged gifts and watched *A Christmas Story*.

We gave Sonia a gold cross pendant and Eugene a fleece jacket that he pulled over his head practically before it was unwrapped. They gifted us with finely woven blue and white baskets with cone shaped covers, handmade by a friend of theirs from Africa.

I wasn't sure what Sonia and Eugene would think of our movie choice, but *A Christmas Story* was one of our favorites. It didn't matter how many times we saw Flick stick his tongue to the flagpole on the heels of a triple dog dare; it was hilarious every time. Although Sonia and Eugene didn't laugh as much as we did, Sonia mentioned one of the scenes three years later, so they must've been at least a little amused. Or something.

When they left, I ran through my usual checklist: Did they seem happy? Were they comfortable? Were my kids friendly enough? By all accounts this evening – with little planning and no fuss – was a success.

My relationship with Sonia continued to grow without much effort on my part. I visited her when our schedules permitted. We talked about the details of our lives, what our jobs were like, what TV shows we watched. We laughed more.

Eugene's reserved personality, on the other hand, made it difficult to know where we stood with him, but we persisted in our efforts to win over his affection and trust. To that end, the girls and I agreed to take Eugene and Jean Pierre sledding on a day we all had off from school.

We arrived at Eugene and Sonia's house with a bag bursting with snow pants, wool socks, boots, knit hats and thick gloves that warmed your hands while immobilizing them at the same time. I opened the bag and handed out the items like Christmas gifts.

"These are to keep you warm," I said. "We're going sledding. You'll get wet and cold if you don't wear them." Jean Pierre held up the snow pants against his body for comparison before pulling them over his jeans. Eugene took a pair and moseyed into his room without saying a word. He reappeared five minutes later, wearing the snow pants.

"This is going to be fun, Eugene!" I said with a trace of laughter in my voice. "Have you ever been sledding before?"

"No," Eugene answered. I looked at Jean Pierre.

"Yes – Mount Kilimanjaro."

"Really? That must have been scary." Jean Pierre shrugged his shoulders.

"Eugene, you're going to have so much fun," Rachel chimed in. Sydney raised an eyebrow. I did a quick tally: one professional sledder, one with zero experience (and maybe less enthusiasm), and three intermediates. *This will be fun if it kills me.*

The five of us piled into my car. In under fifteen minutes we arrived at Neutaconkanut Hill – an abandoned ski area just outside Providence. Although the temperature hovered near freezing, the sun's glare put up a good fight against the brisk air. Several cars occupied the lot, but it was far from full. The hill stood about a hundred yards from where we parked. A blanket of emerald green pine trees enveloped the entire mountain except the cleared path, which led up to its menacing peak. Sledders came into view only as they were losing momentum at the base of the hill.

We trekked through the dense snow, following our breath, sleds in hand. Once the hill was in our field of sight, we watched others make their descent from only midway up, where the earth bent to form a more serious incline. The elements of nature collaborated to create a firm icy covering on the ground, making the uphill climb tricky. We grabbed onto trees and jabbed our toes into the snow, trying to gain a whit of traction. That didn't work. We slid back down several times. Feeling like rats on a treadmill, we struggled to gain forward momentum. Quads burning, we laughed at each other. And ourselves.

I was still focused on the ground beneath my feet when Jean Pierre headed toward the peak, Eugene a few yards behind.

One father standing on the landing halfway up the hill caught my eye.

"That's pretty dangerous," he said shooting a look toward the boys.

"I don't think I can stop them," I shouted back. The defensiveness in my tone surprised me. Everyone standing in the seam of the hill waited for Eugene and Jean Pierre to make their descent.

And they waited some more.

Several minutes passed. I yelled to the group halfway up the hill to go down. Who knew how long it would take for Eugene and Jean Pierre to collect their courage.

Drained of patience, the girls and I went down next. We laughed and screamed at the same time as the rush of adrenaline swept across us with the cold air.

Rock hard snow ramps made by our predecessors dotted the base of the hill. I remembered making these ramps when I was a kid. My parents' driveway dipped into our backyard forming the ideal sledding hill. It appeared humongous to my youthful eyes. My brother and I spent hours moving snow from other parts of the yard to create ramps that would send us soaring across our backyard.

This hill was much bigger, the ramps less forgiving. The man-made inclines tossed me in the air. I felt my brain jiggle each time the earth caught me on my descent. I was afraid of how painful it would be for Eugene who would gather much more speed on his way down. I said a quick prayer that the boys would make it down safely; no concussions, no broken limbs.

As I walked back toward the slope, I saw Jean Pierre poised for takeoff. In a flash, he came sailing down the mountain, Eugene riding his tailwind. Jean Pierre was beaming, his wide grin exposing his egg-white teeth. My eyes moved quickly from Jean Pierre's face to Eugene's. His eyebrows shot up and his lips stretched horizontally in pure terror. Nervous for him, I didn't know whether to laugh or cry.

On one hand, I was grateful to see emotion in Eugene's face – even if it was mostly fear. His adrenaline was rushing and his heart was pounding. These were good sensations for a teenage boy, no? If not now, then maybe later, he would see this as a thrill. It would be one of those bonding adventures, something to talk about long after resting heart rate was restored.

On the other hand, the maternal part of me felt guilty for putting him in harm's way and finding humor in the situation. I was, after all, trying to earn the boy's trust. If he did actually get hurt, I would never forgive myself. Lucky for both of us, he survived the trip. He even decided to go back up the hill. But only halfway.

10

Spring Into Summer

"I thought, 'What the heck is this, America or what?' Going to school and working is tough. I thought I would just go to school first, then work." -Eugene

By spring, Sonia and Eugene's lives were in full swing. Sonia was cleaning rooms at the Newport hotel where her brother worked and taking an English class at a community college. Eugene dedicated himself to his schoolwork during the week. His job, with its commute, devoured his weekends.

Eugene's ESL teacher, Miss Becky, kept popping up in my conversations with him, and not in a good way. Miss Becky had disappeared from Riverdell in the middle of the year, and we had assumed she was gone for good. A couple months later she returned, and Eugene seemed to be getting along with her. I could tell from the number of times he was bringing up her name that the situation was deteriorating – again.

"She doesn't like me. She hates me," he said one afternoon when I prompted him for details. We were sitting in his dark living room, curtains drawn, air conditioner blasting. I was tired from a full day at school, and my mind wandered to the tasks I still needed to complete before my nine o'clock bedtime: make dinner, grade tests, return a phone call, plan my classes. Determined to unravel the situation, I reeled in my thoughts. Otherwise, I stood no chance of helping him.

"Eugene, why wouldn't she like you? Did you do something to make her mad?"

"No! I don't know why she doesn't like me," he insisted, avoiding my eyes as he always did when the conversation turned serious. "She gets mad at me and sends me out of the class to the principal's office." He fiddled with the papers on the coffee table. I grabbed the remote and turned down the TV.

"And you didn't do anything to make her upset?"

"No. She just doesn't like me, but it's fine," he said.

"She just doesn't like you?" I thought he might realize how preposterous his words sounded if I echoed them back.

"No, she likes the Spanish kids. She hates black kids."

I was at a loss. Who knew frustration and compassion could thrive side by side?

It was close to the end of the school year, and Eugene assured me he could survive the remaining weeks with Miss Becky. Next year he would have a new ESL teacher, or so we thought.

We began our summer the same way we had the previous three. As soon as school was out, we packed and headed for Hidden Village in Eastham, a small town on the narrow end of Cape Cod. Tucked away on eighteen acres of pine forest, the seven contemporary rustic cottages that comprised Hidden Village provided the ideal vacation spot for those who cherished their privacy but loved to be near the ocean. My week on the Cape was the highlight of my year. I looked forward to it for months.

Mother Nature was not our friend that summer. The sun made only a rare appearance. Experience had taught us to prepare for these situations. We brought board games and cards, listened to music, and tried to enjoy each other's company. And we did – we really did enjoy being together without any distractions from the outside world. For a while.

It wasn't the first time Wayne and I used the weather as an excuse to check out real estate on our favorite piece of land, but it would be the last.

We fell in love with one particular house in Brewster. I was excited but nervous to share the news with my parents who were coming to stay with us for a couple days at the end of the week. It was tradition. They'd come with us to the beach, then spend the evening with the girls while Wayne and I enjoyed ourselves in Provincetown.

There was nothing like Provincetown in the summertime. Funky shops, tourists and drag queens, all set against a picturesque backdrop of sea and sand. I loved it all. Wayne, in his collared plaid shirt, was an irresistible target for the high-heeled men wearing lipstick and earrings looking for someone to poke fun at. He couldn't have minded because he continued to dress that way even after I bought him a stylish black shirt, which I nicknamed his "P-town" shirt.

The second day of my parents' visit, they filled us in on all they had done with the girls while we were in P-town. Swing dancing to country music and going to Sundae School for ice cream were the main events this year.

"Sydney has to get the same flavor ice cream as her sister," Dad said, his mouth quirked with humor.

"Yup," I confirmed. Rain pelted the windows as we huddled around the fireplace. We sat on hard wooden chairs covered with avocado-green vinyl cushions that, with a trace of humidity, would stick to your thighs. The privacy of this place was a great appeal, but the furnishings were not suited for long hours indoors.

"Sydney scared me last night," Dad said. He was sitting at the kitchen table, his long legs folded beneath him. "After she and Rachel went to bed, she started screaming. A tiny spider was on her window. It was so small, I could barely see it. I went to get it and she screamed, 'No, Grandpa, don't kill it!'" Dad was enjoying himself but Sydney wasn't. She sat at the table next to him, her lips puckered with annoyance. She knew better than to interrupt her grandfather, as much as she wanted to. The irony *was humorous*, though. Who would guess that an animal-loving environmentalist would be terrorized by earth's smallest creatures?

Eventually, I told my parents we'd been house hunting that week. I anticipated a worried look from Dad who was the most conservative person I knew when it came to money. His expression was a mix of concern and intrigue. He asked a lot of questions, and I thought we might've told him too soon. After all, we hadn't made a decision. We were *just looking*.

"Do you need some money?" Mom asked. Typical. Ready to give her money away just like that.

"No, Mom. We're not going to do this if we can't afford to."

"I can give you some money. Why wait until I die? Then I won't be around to see you enjoy it." Again. Typical.

Later that day, we drove to the Brewster house with my parents. We peeked in the windows and explored the yard. Dad seemed skeptical, like it wasn't much house for the amount they were asking. But we knew otherwise. We had seen a lot of houses that week.

That evening, the six of us went to our favorite seafood restaurant. It was a big clam shack really, unpretentious and informal, where they served the best fried seafood and onion rings alongside more sophisticated, and equally scrumptious, seafood entrees and salads. Inside they had a mini-bar where they served fresh shellfish and beer. Outside, teenagers doled out monstrous portions of homemade ice cream to tourists, bikers and residents alike. A food paradise for someone like me who craved sugar and salt in equal measures.

The owners had recently added a miniature golf course to their venue – as if they were aiming for a grown-ups' version of Disney World. Miniature golf, or "putt-putt" as we called it, was another family tradition. My parents took my brother and me to play every year when we were on the Cape, and now a summer never slipped by without us taking Rachel and Sydney. It was a no-brainer that we were going to play here.

We weren't even halfway through the game when the skies again opened. Rain came slowly at first. Caught up in one of our favorite vacation pastimes, egos on the line, we barely noticed. Then it poured. The wind sucked our only umbrella inside out until it was beyond repair. The rain lashed out at our bare legs as we sloshed through the course, but we kept playing. Scores were close; it was anyone's game.

The twelfth hole was directly in front of the restaurant's window. Amused eyes stared out at my saturated family, making us all too aware of how foolish we looked. Finally, Wayne called it.

Like pouting children, we conceded to his wisdom and scurried inside. We looked out the broad window and realized how funny we must've looked to those seated in the dining room. People tried not to stare at us, but some couldn't help themselves. We felt like celebrities of a tacky reality show.

Lunch tasted so good after that.

We did some number crunching and, ultimately, a good interest rate and buyer's market convinced us to buy the Brewster house. Wayne and I had plenty of financial discussions, but there was never any question that *this particular house* suited us perfectly. Although this had been a life-long dream, the decision felt impulsive and risky, maybe a little naughty – like my husband and I were two teenagers trying not to get caught skipping school to hide in our secret club-house.

We closed in mid-August in Barnstable, a town that sits at the western end of the Cape. As soon as the papers were signed, Wayne took the girls home to Rhode Island. I headed straight to the new house. My plan was to get some painting done before moving in the truckloads of furniture we had recently purchased on Craigslist. I called Mom as soon as I arrived at the house. I was giddy, like a child with her heart's desires unleashed.

"I'm so happy!" I piped into the phone.

"I know you are," she said. And she did. She knew better than anyone.

Oh, to own a piece of land on my favorite peninsula. I vowed to never take this gift for granted, but I also felt guilty for feeling so fiercely attached to *a place*. I was in love with it, really. When I was not near it, I longed for its sights and smells. In its presence, I was a calmer, happier, kinder version of myself.

I couldn't sleep that first night, no matter how much I tried. I lay in bed wide-eyed, thoughts racing, like a child antic-ipating a trip to Hersheypark. I decided to end the torture. Around two in the morning, I turned on all the lights and continued the painting I had started earlier that evening. Just me, my Cape house, and the orchestra of tree frogs outside my window. It didn't matter that I had owned this place for only a few hours. *I was home.*

The cottage was modest, with about 1200 square feet of living space. The layout (kitchen downstairs, living room upstairs) would appear strange to some, but to me it was reminiscent of my grandparents' house on the hill. When I first entered the cottage with our realtor, my mind raced to Mémère's basement kitchen and insisted on lingering there. It had served as my family's retreat once the sun went down and mosquitoes began to swarm. The grown-ups would sit downstairs in the kitchen, drinking and smoking, while the kids ran around upstairs in the living room making as much noise as they wanted. It was perfect really. And this house was, too.

From the outside, the cottage looked like a traditional Cape Cod house, its gray shingles and cream-colored trim worn by the weather and salt. The roof extended over the side door, providing just enough shade for two wooden rocking chairs. The yard was home to a small but bountiful garden and a shed adorned with curtains and flower boxes. It didn't have a water view (unless you count the swamp it abutted) and it didn't sit on a five-acre wooded lot; it didn't have a screened-in porch, a deck, patio, or fireplace. But it was more than we ever dreamed of. It was on Cape Cod.

The girls and I spent our final two weeks of summer there. I vowed to make the most of my time on this stretch of land, which simultaneously filled my soul and emptied my mind of anxious thoughts. This would be the perfect medicine to prepare myself for the onslaught of another school year.

About two weeks before the start of school, in late August, I received a call from Eugene.

"I got my schedule, Chris. I have Miss Becky again. I don't

want to have Miss Becky." He sounded definite. "Maybe you can get me out of the class?" Eugene didn't ask for much, so when he did ask me for something, I paid close attention.

"OK, Eugene." I tried to reassure him. "I'll call your guidance counselor and see what I can do." I knew this meant several phone calls and possibly a visit to the school. I didn't tell him I was speaking to him from my new house on the Cape.

As I prepared to return to Rhode Island, tension crept into every corner of my body. All my soul's progress was coming undone with the mere thought of leaving. My mind, which had been gaining clearer perspective, was drifting off course and my spirit was starting to droop. Like a child tearing off a Band-Aid, I found it best to make the departure as quick as possible.

I drove to Riverdell High School soon after returning to the mainland. Back-to-school ads were in full bloom, but it was my visit to Eugene's high school that brought the start of a new school year into full view, before I was ready to even think about sharpening my pencils.

Riverdell High School sat in a residential neighborhood in west Providence. Built in the sixties, the enormous brick building had an old majestic look to it. I walked in the front entrance and asked a janitor to direct me to the guidance office. The halls were much wider than the ones at Moses Brown, and I couldn't help but picture what they'd look like when the thousand students returned. I had a funny habit of counting desks when in schools other than MB, and the classes at Riverdell had almost twice as many seats as what I can fit in my classroom. I tried to visualize what it would be like to have so many students in front of me, coming from so many different backgrounds with so many different levels of aspirations. I wondered if I could be an effective teacher in this school. The answer I landed on was no; I should stay put and leave the tough teaching to those better suited than me.

My thoughts returned to Eugene when I arrived at the guidance office. I introduced myself to the receptionist, and she phoned Eugene's counselor who promptly came out to greet me. The middle-aged woman with dyed black hair politely outlined the many details that went into making the students' schedules. She spoke highly of Miss Becky, suggesting that the problem was with Eugene.

"I know he can be stubborn," I admitted, "but this is not a good match for either of them. If there is any way to switch him into the other class, I think everyone would be better off."

I'm sure she gave some reasonable explanation for why this couldn't happen, but all I heard was, "It's very difficult because... blah, blah, blah..."

She never said no, but I left with a strong sense that Eugene would be spending another year with Miss Becky. He was not going to be happy, and neither was I. I failed to help Eugene the one time he had asked – the one time it mattered.

I was not naïve enough to think Eugene was completely blameless in the mounting tension between him and Miss Becky. As mild mannered and reserved as he was, Eugene had a strong will. And forgiveness was not one of his strengths.

I had met several of Eugene's friends, but he held onto only a few. When I'd ask about this one or that one, he'd give me a curt answer, the gist of which was that the former friend had not lived up to Eugene's expectations. I remember one boy in particular whom I had met when I volunteered to meet a group of refugees at the airport to help transport them to their new apartment. This boy, Peter, was from Rwanda and also there to help. He had an easy-going personality and I liked him instantly. By the end of the night, we were teasing each other like old friends. When I brought his name up to Eugene, he told me Peter was bad.

"What do you mean?" I asked.

"He can't keep a job. He was working on Block Island and he got fired," Eugene explained. "He's not good."

"He was homeless for a while," Sonia added.

"Really?" It didn't seem like we could be talking about the same person.

Their reaction gave me a flash of insight into their values. They had no empathy for someone whose situation was a result of their own bad decisions.

I never again mentioned his name.

PART II

Choppy Waters

11

Another School Year

"When I lost my job, I thought, 'forget it, I'll find another one.' I didn't think it was a big deal to lose your job in America. I thought it would still be OK." –Eugene

As a new school year took hold, I spun through my usual cycle of emotions, eventually settling somewhere between resignation and mild enthusiasm. My mind focused on school and exercise. And Eugene.

His tutor, Kyle, had graduated, and I was determined to find someone to fill the void he left in Eugene's life. The boys had a special bond, and Eugene was going to miss his friend.

I was confident I could find another tutor for Eugene, one he'd like. I didn't have time to research students' schedules ahead of time, so I tried a different approach.

After explaining the connection between limits and continuity to my AP Calculus class one day, I wrote the home-work assignment on the board. This signaled the end of class to my students, who initially found it disconcerting not to have a clock in sight. The only teacher without one, I feared it would transform them into zombie teens, obsessed with the number of minutes until I released them to their friends and cell phones. Without a clock, maybe I could erase time in my classroom, allow students to surrender to their intellectual curiosity and soak up everything I had to offer. Sure, that could work.

The shuffling of backpacks and cumulative whispers created an energetic sound, breaking the silence of my students' attention. When I began to explain Eugene's situation, the chatter stopped and I could feel all eyes refocusing on me. It was the beginning of the school year, and I hadn't yet developed close relationships with my students. Their sudden silence and serious expressions unsettled me, and I could hear the nervousness in my voice. I explained that I was seeking one or two people to help Eugene with his homework each week.

"I can help, but not until cross country season is over," one student offered.

"I think I can. I have to talk to my parents," said a girl with wide rimmed glasses and a pointy nose.

"I'm available, but I don't have a car," another explained. At this point, several students were moving toward me.

"I can help in the fall, but I'm not sure I'll have time in the winter because of basketball," another added. I grabbed a piece of paper and recorded the information. I hoped to piece together a schedule that would work for my students and Eugene. More than half the group expressed a desire to tutor Eugene, but I had hoped to find someone who was available through the winter. I couldn't fault them for their busy schedules. I was grateful that so many wanted to help.

As others were leaving, David, a quiet student who sat in the back, came forward.

"I'm available every day and I have a car," he said.

"Really?" I asked. I thought this was too good to be true. "Great." I decided not to question my good fortune.

The tension between Eugene and Miss Becky was gathering steam. She sent him out of her room on a regular basis, causing him to miss up to three hours of his ESL class a day. I couldn't imagine what behavior warranted this consequence. Eugene didn't provide specifics, just insisted Miss Becky hated him. Wayne and I decided to settle the matter once and for all.

Wayne set up a meeting with Miss Becky, the vice-principal of Riverdell High School, and Eugene. Not an easy task. Meetings after school or during lunch were not an option, so it had to be during Miss Becky's free period. The culture at Moses Brown was different. Teachers often gave up their lunch periods or stayed after school to meet with students or parents. But we had fewer students under our care. I could only imagine how many students Miss Becky saw each day.

The meeting took place on a brisk December afternoon. Wayne had just returned to Providence after a meeting in Cambridge. Though he'd never been to Riverdell High, he quickly stumbled upon the vice-principal's office, small and windowless. Wayne exchanged greetings with Vice-Principal Tim McCormick, the person he had spoken to on the phone. Tim was shorter than he had imagined, with a pale complexion. Moments later, Miss Becky and Eugene arrived. Miss Becky was an older woman, sixtyish, also small in stature, with silvery gray hair. Her crinkled brows and tight lips gave her a defensive look, like she was readying for combat.

Wayne began the conversation, expressing his desire to find out what was going on in the classroom and to come up with an agreeable solution. Tim returned his friendly attitude and seemed eager to resolve the conflict between Eugene and Miss Becky.

Miss Becky explained that Eugene had been misbehaving in class, acting up and not paying attention. This was out of character for Eugene, so Wayne could only assume there was more to the story from Eugene's perspective. Eugene slouched in his chair, tilted his head to the floor. Wayne guessed he was embarrassed to be the center of their conversation.

"Remember the time you made me cry?" Miss Becky asked Eugene, who acknowledged her with a subtle nod.

"What happened?" Wayne scooted his chair forward.

"One day Eugene was walking around the classroom, yelling and screaming, 'This is so stupid! This is so stupid!'" Miss Becky was visibly upset as if she was reliving the scene in her mind. "He wouldn't sit down or listen to me, so I sent him to the office."

Wayne was caught off guard with this new information, but surmised that something had caused Eugene to lose his temper. Wayne told Miss Becky that Eugene felt she didn't like him, but she claimed she had no ill feelings toward Eugene. Either way, his behavior in her classroom was unacceptable.

As if he didn't know what else to do, Tim asked Eugene if he'd agree to stop misbehaving in Miss Becky's class and Eugene complied.

"I'll check in from time to time," Tim promised, "just to make sure."

So that was it. All that mystery and drama and it was over – like an unsatisfying movie that ends mid-plot while you're still trying to figure out what's happening. I hate those movies.

In later conversations, Eugene indicated things were better in Miss Becky's class, and I was glad. I knew better than to expect details. Of course, he could've just been trying to avoid another uncomfortable meeting.

While Eugene was starting a new school year, Sonia was starting a new job. The long commute from Newport had made it impossible for her to take an evening ESL course. She had been looking for another housekeeping job closer to her apartment, and she eventually found one. It wasn't a dream job by any means, but the location made her schedule more manageable.

I wanted to show Sonia how happy I was for her, and that fate was finally on her side. So one weekday afternoon, while Rachel and Sydney were playing sports, I popped into a flower shop near school to buy her a gift. I chose a tall white orchid that looked appropriately strong and feminine. The flower would convey my excitement better than my words. Of this I was certain.

When the girls and I arrived at their apartment, Eugene greeted us with a perplexed look. He studied the confident looking plant in my arms as I walked past him at the doorway. I sat on the sofa and set my gift on the coffee table. Eugene's fixation with it prompted my explanation.

"This is for Sonia, to congratulate her on her new job." I wasn't sure if Eugene even knew about the change.

"How much did it cost?" he asked with a disapproving tone.

"Not much," I assured him, though he didn't look like he believed me.

"Is Sonia home?" I asked.

"She's in the kitchen."

The girls and I followed the pungent spices to the back of the house where Sonia was cooking dinner. Enthusiastically, I presented her with my token of pride. She thanked me in a fragile voice, though she didn't appear as joyous about her new job as I expected. Or the plant.

"What did your employer say when you told him you found another job?" I asked. Sonia's blank stare unnerved me, told me something was amiss.

"Did you tell him?" Her dispassion suddenly made sense. I had told Sonia that it was customary to give two weeks' notice before quitting, so I was confused by her decision not to. "Why didn't you tell him, Sonia?" I sensed I was starting to sound pushy.

"I thought maybe I could wait and try out the new job first. That way, if I don't like it, I can go back to my old job," she said, letting her voice trail off.

"You can't do that, Sonia." Still, I understood her rationale. What if she didn't like working at the new hotel? She had so much to lose. Of course she was afraid to quit her job without knowing what the new one was like. I tried to convince her everything was going to work out with her new job, that it's what she had wanted.

Sonia explained that the job developer from the International Institute had a different opinion. She thought Sonia was unwise to give up a position in a hotel that the Institute had a relationship with. Other employers might not be as patient or understanding with a refugee worker. No wonder Sonia felt conflicted.

The following week, Sonia explained her situation to her employer in Newport (who was understanding) and switched jobs. In January she enrolled in a class at the local community college and scheduled her work hours around her class. Finally the pieces of her life were arranging themselves sensibly.

Sonia also found a driving instructor and was studying to pass the driver's test. She had failed it once before, and I had made the mistake of slipping the information to her brother, assuming he already knew. Eugene couldn't stop laughing.

"I will pass mine the first try," he said with a smile that wouldn't leave his face.

Eugene, Sonia and Emmanuel moved again that fall, but only down the street. Robert had found them a more modern apartment for slightly more money. Sonia would have her own bathroom. Its layout was similar to their previous apartment, but the kitchen and living space were combined.

David, Eugene's tutor, helped with the move, which was almost complete by the time I arrived with the girls after school. I was not disappointed. It seemed like we had just moved them, and now they had a lot more stuff. Besides items that were given to them (air conditioner, microwave, beds), they had an assortment of new purchases: flat-screen TV, computer and printer, several high-back pink cushioned chairs.

I was happy they were building a comfortable home for themselves, but concerned about how much they were spending.

Not everyone thought about money the way I did. Some people spent what they had, assuming they'd get by. Others, like myself, planned for the worst. If I were in Sonia and Eugene's shoes, I would've been stashing away as much as possible, just in case.

My concern about their financial situation skyrocketed that evening when Wayne told me he had stumbled across a bank statement showing that Eugene had taken out a fifteen-hundred-dollar loan. We never asked him about it, but I often wondered what he had used the money for. I was careful not to overstep. I didn't want to risk pushing Eugene away.

Stress poured into Eugene and Sonia's lives that fall when

Eugene lost his job. He gave us some confusing explanation that I don't remember. Once again, we were left without details. He sent me an email: "I am going crazy in my head. I don't know what to do. But it's OK. Love you. Eugene." Eugene's e-mails always caused a visceral reaction in me, making me want to jump up and help him.

I showed Eugene how to search for jobs on Craigslist and how to reply to ones he was interested in. I created a resume for him and showed him how to attach it to his e-mails. I wasn't sure how much he understood or remembered. As someone who needs repetition for something to sink in – especially when it comes to technology – I didn't assume that Eugene was going to master everything I showed him right away.

Whenever I asked him how his search was going, he'd say, "It's not easy." I didn't know what that meant. Did he need more help? Was he filling out applications and not getting responses? My gut told me he wasn't doing much. And my reaction bounced from frustration to guilt. On one hand, I was frustrated with him for not being more proactive. On the other, I felt guilty for not taking the time to find out exactly what was thwarting his progress. Was it something I could help him with? If I didn't know, I could maintain my distance, stay on my fast-moving treadmill called life with blinders secure. What kind of a person did that make me?

On top of the financial stress, or perhaps because of it, a wall was growing between Sonia and Eugene. Eugene wasn't confiding in me, but Sonia was. According to her, they were arguing a lot, mainly about money.

"He gets mad when I say something, but he keeps spending money," Sonia told me one afternoon when I stopped by her apartment. She handed me a cable bill with several twelve-dollar movie charges. "Look. He and Jean Pierre have been getting movies." I looked closer at the piece of paper, glanced at the movie titles. Yes, Eugene and Jean Pierre had been watching adult movies that neither of them could afford.

Although Sonia was only a year older than her brother, she carried a parent's burden without the leverage. She felt responsible for Eugene's safety and well-being, but powerless to control him.

"He never had a parent to tell him what to do," was her explanation for Eugene's behavior. Although he didn't have parents, Eugene was fortunate to have Sonia.

At the peak of Sonia's annoyance with Eugene, Wayne agreed to have a man-to-man talk with him. One weekday evening he brought Eugene to a nearby Wendy's restaurant. The dining room was empty except for a handful of people. Eugene and Wayne sat across from one another at a mustard-colored booth in the corner of the dining room.

"I want to help you find a job," Wayne began. "But you need to make an effort, too."

Eugene nodded without looking up. "I know, but it's not easy." He fed Wayne the same line I had heard many times.

"I know, Eugene, but you can pick up applications from McDonald's, CVS, and other places in your neighborhood. Then I'll help you fill them out."

"OK," Eugene said in a resigned voice. He sipped his soda.

"On the way home, I'll drive you around and point out the places you should go to this week," Wayne continued.

"OK," Eugene repeated.

When they finished their meal, the pair walked to the car in silence. They drove through the dark neighborhood, mapping out the route Eugene would take on his own later that week.

"Call me when you have the applications," Wayne reminded Eugene as he dropped him off in front of his apartment.

"Yes. Thank you," he said tersely.

Days passed. Wayne never heard from Eugene about the applications.

12

Mom

In New England, Thanksgiving marks the gateway to winter. The trees, once trimmed in gold and crimson, gradually shed their colorful layers, covering the ground with a blanket of autumn hues. The cool crisp air holds the aroma of dried leaves, signaling the impending arrival of colder temperatures.

My family looked forward to this American tradition, but Thanksgiving was not my favorite holiday. While I enjoyed spending time with loved ones, much of the day was devoted to cooking and cleaning – two of my least favorite activities.

I couldn't complain. It's not like I had to cook for an army. We usually had just my parents over, sometimes my brother. This year, however, our table would be fuller. Wayne's dad, Eugene, and Sonia would also join us.

No surprise that my parents arrived early, arms loaded with

bags of chips, homemade clam dip, sweets for the girls, a pie pan I had left at their house – and some Jody Picoult books for the bookshelves in our Cape house. My parents never came empty-handed.

As soon as our dog, Sparkey, eyed Dad walking up the driveway, he began barking and wagging his tail in unison. Dad extended his hand to Sparkey and spoke to him in a forceful voice that only escalated my dog's anxiety.

"Oh, Joe, leave the poor dog alone. You're scaring him," Mom said.

Dad kept chatting with the dog, who I'm guessing took issue with Dad's height as well as his friendly roar.

Both my parents were tall, but Mom was rounder than Dad. Her weight had always been her archenemy. To me, she looked beautiful. Her hair, which was once thick and black, was thinning and gray like Dad's. But that only accentuated her high cheekbones and smooth skin. I had always wished I had her skin.

The quiet part of our day ended with dog barking, Dad hollering at dog, Mom reeling off instructions regarding what she had brought. My parents always arrived with a blast. Wayne's dad, Houston, who had flown in the day before, drifted into the kitchen to greet my parents.

Short in stature with flaxen hair, Houston was a mild-mannered southern gentleman. He and my parents didn't see each other often, but when they did, they acted like old friends. I herded them into the sunroom, away from my tiny cooking space. I hated small talk almost as much as I hated cooking. I didn't need to be doing both at once.

Wayne returned minutes later with Eugene and Sonia while I was scrambling to synchronize the meal. Timing is the real challenge of cooking all those side dishes, isn't it? I paused to greet them and hoped they didn't notice the angst behind my smile. It's not that I had anything new to fret about – just the worry that everyone would have a miserable time and it would be my fault. Different day, same anxieties.

Wayne brought Eugene and Sonia into the sunroom, and introduced them to our parents. Then he joined me in the kitchen and we teamed up to push the meal to the finish line. We were pretty good at that, though I tried to do more than my share beforehand so I wouldn't feel guilty slacking off when guests arrived. It was part of my stress management plan. Wayne was better at social multi-tasking. Our system gave Mom the wrong impression.

Mom adored Wayne. She often told me how lucky I was to have him. One Thanksgiving as we were finishing our meal, she said, "Wayne, everything was so delicious. And you did this all by yourself!" I looked at Wayne, waited for him to correct her, but he didn't. Mom's reverence for Wayne convinced me she believed I was the one in the marriage who hit the jackpot. It bothered me for a long time. When I tired of feeling sorry for myself, I recognized the hilarity of the situation. After all, it could have been much worse: She could've despised him.

We were in the last stretch of preparing the meal. I mashed potatoes, Wayne opened a can of gravy. I reached up to heat my pre-cooked sweet potatoes in the microwave and Wayne, checking the turkey, bumped me. I scowled at him. Then

I stepped back, breathed in the smells of our Thanksgiving feast and sipped my wine. That's what I was forgetting – to drink my wine.

I apologized to my husband.

"I hope they're including Eugene and Sonia in the conversation," I said.

"Don't worry," Wayne said.

He was right. I *had* prepped my daughters and needn't visualize the worst case scenario. This was something I had to work at.

Some days were better than others.

Luckily, I only found out later that Mom had pressed Eugene about his job, not realizing he had been fired. I cringed at the thought of Eugene's discomfort.

Later in the afternoon, as my parents were preparing to leave, Mom mentioned feeling tired.

"Are you all right?" I asked.

"I haven't been feeling well this week," she finally admitted.

"What's the matter?" I was more curious than concerned at this point.

"Oh, nothing, just a little touch of pneumonia," she said.

"What?" I couldn't believe this was the first I was hearing about it. "Shouldn't you have stayed home and rested?" I realized that our mother-daughter roles had suddenly switched.

"I did rest," she insisted like a teenager with a bit of attitude. "I just sat all day. That was resting."

I was annoyed by her pigheadedness, but not at all surprised.

"Well, go home and relax," I urged her.

"I will," she promised with a serious look, trying to take away my worry.

The next day, we threw clothes in duffle bags and headed to the Cape. We were eager to settle in for the weekend and show Houston our favorite places. Our first stop was a family-owned home and garden store in Orleans, one town east of Brewster. Having been in business for over a hundred years, it was a local landmark. Tempting sales lured in customers on this early shopping day. Christmas carols piped in through large speakers while a toy train chugged around the store's perimeter.

I was starting to absorb the spirit of my favorite holiday when my cell phone rang. It was Dad. Mom had been hospitalized. Her symptoms had become intolerable, and the doctors discovered that an accumulation of fluid inside her stomach was the culprit. They were able to drain it, Dad explained, and she felt better instantly. They would need to run a series of tests to determine the cause of the fluid build-up. I left my family and drove to Worcester that night. In less than two hours, I was striding into the hospital room. An alert and cheery Mom greeted me, and I was relieved.

I spent the night at Dad's house and visited Mom again the next day. That evening, when I pulled into my driveway back in Rhode Island, my family was emptying out of the Mazda. They had decided not to stay on the Cape without me, and I was heartened to see them.

Shortly afterwards the phone rang. Mom's voice on the

other end surprised me since I had left her a few hours earlier. I don't remember much of the conversation. I think it was a short one. What I do remember were the three words: "I have cancer." There was no drama in her voice, no emotion. The news bulleted through me, paralyzed me for I don't know how long. Then the reality poured over me like a rogue wave that would eventually knock me to my knees. At that moment, I hated the doctor who gave her the news – not for turning my world upside down – but for telling Mom at night when she had no family to help absorb the blow.

Mom started her chemotherapy almost immediately. At first, she handled the side effects well and it seemed like our worst nightmare wasn't actually happening. Mom's outlook was optimistic. I remember how excited she was about going wig shopping with her friend.

"Can you believe that my insurance will pay for this?" The spark in her voice almost brushed away my fear. From that day on, our moods were tied to how well her body was reacting to and tolerating the only medicine that could prolong her life.

Some days were great. "I had to tell you as soon as I heard – my cancer count is down to three hundred!"

Other days were not as hopeful. "I had to postpone my treatment because my white blood cell count was too low. But, I'm going to eat a lot of liver, because that's supposed to help!"

Mom was like a soldier gearing up for battle: She was going to fight this disease with every weapon she had.

Christmas snuck up on me the year of Mom's diagnosis. Usually Christmas-related thoughts flowed in and out of my consciousness for several months. For one, there were many holiday decisions to make: what presents to buy, whether to send Christmas cards with or without photos, how to spend the week I had off between Christmas and New Year's. And then there was the anticipation of seeing my entire extended family at my parents' house on Christmas Eve. There'd be talk of which cousins from the west coast would come, and whether or not my elusive cousin David would make an appearance. The success of the party was measured by how many relatives showed up.

I'm not saying I had a perfect family, or that we at all resembled the Cleavers. No, we had several loud voices and the alcohol flowed freely when we were together. We were not always on our best behavior around our kids. But we genuinely loved each other's company and had a blast together. Lots of hugs, laughter and friendly razzing (and bad singing on occasion). So the news that Mom wasn't going to host or attend the event, due to a high risk of infection, cast a shadow over our holiday. This was on all our minds weeks before the party.

Mom was the oldest of five children, and her siblings were each born five years apart. I was the second oldest of my generation, born only eleven months after my brother. From my perspective, we had a young family. After my grandmother died, Mom inherited the role of matriarch and became the glue that kept the family together. She thrived in this position, relishing the attention and esteem it held. Giving up her seat at the helm was not easy for her the first Christmas Eve after her diagnosis. Nevertheless, she conceded to my Aunt Jayne with the condition that she would "have it back" the following year.

A sense of gloom hung in the air as my family made the hour-long drive to my parents' house, before going to the Christmas Eve party at my aunt's. I felt like I was holding grief in one hand while trying to hold up joy and gratitude in the other. Unsettled by the break in our long-standing tradition, I felt less tethered to the earth than I was a year ago. I thought of Eugene and Sonia and how they must have felt losing both their parents at such a young age. And then moving to a different continent. If I felt untethered, they must've felt like satellites spinning out of orbit.

I spoke with Sonia often about Mom, and she shared stories of hers. She never let on that her losses were greater than mine, although they were – without a doubt. Instead, she acknowledged my pain like a true friend, with empathy and kindness. Eugene did, too, in his own way. He and I communicated frequently through e-mail, and his messages were filled with affection and humor.

When we arrived at my parents' home on the outskirts of Worcester, Mom and Dad were in good spirits, acting as though our visit was all that mattered. Mom wore a festive red sweater with a pair of black pants. A blue knit cap covered her head, and I was thankful she wasn't wearing one of her wigs. I hated the way Mom looked in her wigs. To me, she was beautiful with or without hair, but I couldn't stand the sight of either of those thick gray wigs. Mom's hair was thinning by the time it turned gray. It went from thick and black to thin and gray. It was never thick and gray.

We sat in the cozy living room furnished with plush oversized furniture. Almost everything – curtains, carpet, walls – was in the same shade of blue or tan. If there was a name for my parents' decorating style, it would be "perfect match." High school portraits of my brother and me hung in the center of the wall. In his photo, my brother had a headful of hair, all combed forward. My hair flipped off my face in large curls, eighties style.

Dad kept the house as tidy as a hotel. He put up only a few Christmas decorations this year. Who could blame him? He had more important matters on his mind

As we were talking, my cousin, Michael, and his fiancée, Lee, came by for a visit. Michael was my mom's godson, and this was not a relationship that either of them took lightly. He proudly presented Mom with a container of pasta he and Lee had made themselves. His thoughtfulness lit up her face.

Michael was not the youngest cousin in my family, but his baby face and quick wit made him everyone's favorite. When I was around ten, my cousin Donna and I would sleep over at my aunt's house so we could dote on him. My aunt would let us help bathe and powder him, hold him to our heart's content – until he started wailing. We carried our maternal roles with him well into his childhood. He was the center of our entertainment when we crossed paths at Mémère's house. Donna and I thought he was the most adorable, funny child who ever lived. When I looked at him now, it wasn't difficult to see the quirky little toddler who once captivated us.

"Look at the time. You better go to Jaynie's. It's almost six," Mom said.

"OK." I knew there was no point in arguing.

"Wish everyone a Merry Christmas for me," Mom said smiling.

"Of course," I said. "I love you." I made a conscious decision to look her straight in the eye as if my words could pierce through the air and touch her soul.

"I love you too," she said, her eyes brimming with strength and emotion.

After our good-byes, we drove to my Aunt Jayne's house, two towns away. Her house was already full with family.

Rachel and Sydney scrambled off to a bedroom with my cousin's girls. In the finished basement, Mom's siblings were settled at the bar, as if they'd been there for a while. I came from a whole family of early arrivers.

A festive energy filled the room.

I remember a conversation I had with my cousin, Christopher.

"You know… your mom is going to be OK. You know that, right?" he said, taking control of a stray hair dangling in his face. I wondered how he could be certain when reams of evidence indicated otherwise. He picked up on my doubt. "Well, she is," he stated definitively, which was oddly comforting even if I didn't believe him.

"Be quiet, everyone!" Uncle David yelled. "We're going to

call Lucy." He put Mom on speakerphone so everyone could wish her a Merry Christmas.

"Merry Christmas," Mom said, her voice cracking.

13

Sonia's News

"I was so scared. I didn't know what I was going to do." -Sonia

Cheetos, Funny Bones and Sam Adams. Salt, sugar and hops – I had my three main food groups. As the register tallied the cost, I passed a crinkled twenty across the counter. Locally made lavender soap, penuche fudge, and five-cent pretzel sticks standing upright in a dingy plastic jar cluttered its surface. I wondered what the long-haired teenage boy on the other side thought of my purchase, or my drenched hair, or my pajamas, which barely passed for sweats. No matter. He had seen me this way before and would undoubtedly see me this way again. The location of this country store (less than a quarter mile from my summer home) made it convenient for me to bop over to satisfy my most fleeting cravings. Tourists flocked to the quaint store down the road, but I preferred this one – with its old-fashioned phone booth, stereo from the seventies and mediocre beer selection. At least it *had* a beer selection.

"No bag, thanks." I grabbed my second dinner, pushed through the screen door and strolled to my car in the empty lot. A conquered triathlon earlier that day was my excuse to indulge. Guilt-free eating was, after all, one of the perks of exercise addiction.

One time, after running a marathon in Arizona, my friend Joyce and I feasted on jelly beans, donuts, Doritos and Snickers bars on the four-hour flight back to Rhode Island. Our fold-out trays disappeared under aluminum and cellophane wrappings while Cajun spices, peanutty chocolate and chewy citrus flavors commingled in our mouths. When the plane landed, we could barely move. I was showing much more restraint on this cool sunny afternoon.

It was the spring of 2010, and I was still in the honeymoon phase of owning a summer house on Cape Cod, a place that held a zillion sparkling childhood memories. Just under two hours from our Rhode Island house, it was ideal for weekend family getaways when schedules permitted. Even better, I could do a solo escape – when stars aligned and the cosmos conceded.

As a teacher, mother and wife, social interactions devoured my time and energy; I craved solitude. Truth is, sporadic retreats to my hermit's hideaway became essential to keeping my mental health barometer in the sanity range. Along with exercise and Prozac.

This was one of my first weekends alone since buying our

cottage in Brewster, and it came on the heels of completing my second triathlon, just a few miles off Cape. A triathlon followed by a weekend of guilt-free eating and drinking alone by the shore – this was pretty much off the Richter scale of awesomeness for me. But as much as I leaned into these tangible forms of pleasure, a heavy heart kept me from relishing this party for one.

I used to think that distance running was a metaphor for life, probably because I had read it somewhere. I was wrong. Life is much more like a triathlon, with distinct stages. And the final performance all boils down to how one handles the transitions.

During the swim leg, for example, the athlete focuses on carrying out the motions she has rehearsed countless times. She is in a routine. She has time to think, plan, and adjust her strategy if necessary. But once out of the water she must, in rapid sequence, peel her wetsuit off her arms, run across the beach, and find her bike among the hundreds, maybe thousands, parked in the transition area. She steps onto her towel, spread neatly beside her bike, and clumsily pulls her wetsuit off her ankles while trying to maintain her balance. She inevitably fumbles, scattering the energy bar, water bottle and running clothes she'd painstakingly arranged on the ground beside her bike with laser-like precision. All that planning turns to chaos in an instant.

A successful triathlon has everything to do with the transitions – that part of the race for which there is no rehearsal. And so it is with life. It's the transitional periods that challenge us, throw us off our game, give us an up close and sometimes not so pleasant look at ourselves.

It was only a matter of time before I would begin a new phase of my life, one that didn't include my mother. Like the triathlete whose small world is suddenly thrown into chaos when she trips over her water bottle, I was struggling to keep the pieces of my comfortable existence from scattering in all directions.

No, I was not handling this transition with grace. Although I wasn't angry with God, I wasn't at all happy with His choices. I had summoned Him ever so sweetly when there was hope He might give me the outcome I wanted. But now that His decision was clear, I ignored Him like a spoiled teenager.

I found myself driving past the road to Saint's Landing beach several times without even a glance in its direction. If I hadn't been alone with my thoughts for so long, I wouldn't have noticed my peculiar behavior. Normally, when I was lucky enough to be this close to the ocean, I would seek its nourishment at least once a day. But this weekend I was avoiding it.

The beach is my spiritual place. For reasons I can't adequately describe, I feel closest to God when I'm alone, looking out at the horizon where sky meets water. Anxiety and insecurities wash away with each receding wave. I fill to the brim with whatever my soul is craving: strength, peace, raw joy. Sometimes even a sense of humor. These are gifts from God, I know, and can be received anywhere. But for me, it all happens by the shore. Today I wasn't ready to be close to God; I was turning a cold shoulder.

It was the next morning when, recovered from the triathlon and feeling physically and mentally re-energized, I slipped on my sandals and drove to the beach, coffee in hand. I sat on the lone bench facing the horizon, dug my toes into the sand. I didn't bother to take in the sounds and smells that greeted me. I barely noticed the rain dripping on my bare arms.

I sat on the bench and watched the ocean slowly empty itself, leaving behind rippled mudflats and cracked seashells. As the drops of rain came down more forcefully, I cried. I asked God to take care of my mother who had been diagnosed with stage-four ovarian cancer.

Then I let the power of this place take hold. When I was ready, as if with the tug of faith on my hand, I walked to my car.

Back at the house, I searched for my cell phone in my oversized butterscotch-yellow purse. Without a landline on the Cape, I had to remind myself to check for messages. For someone who resisted most things technology, this was more difficult than it sounds. Do you know anyone else who carries around a torn address book from the eighties?

I was proud of myself for noticing I had a message from Sonia and for promptly returning her call.

"Hi, Sonia. How are you?"

"I don't know, Chris." Sonia said in a slow Kinyarwanda accent that held a sense of urgency. "I'm all right, but I have something to tell you. I don't want to talk about it now. Not on the phone."

Suddenly distracted from my own troubles, I imagined possible scenarios that would unglue Sonia. She had been laid off from her job since January and had been looking for another one while taking classes toward her CNA (certified nursing assistant) certification. Her crisis was not likely related to work or school. A glance at my watch and quick calculation indicated I had just enough time to stop by her apartment before my doctor's appointment, but only if I left immediately.

"I'm leaving now, Sonia. I'll be there in an hour and a half."

"Yes, that's good. Thank you."

I tossed my wet hair into a ponytail, grabbed my bag of sweaty clothes and flew out the door. I found myself speeding.

"Oh, fuck," I said out loud when the stoplight in front of me turned red. Most of my cursing was confined to the car, and much of it landed on my children's ears. Sydney and Rachel were used to it and hadn't picked up my habit. Not yet, anyway.

I didn't think the kids really noticed until one day when we were trying to leave school in a snowstorm. I couldn't get enough traction to maneuver my car out of the parking lot, and I was furious that school hadn't been cancelled because the weather forecast had been spot on. Not knowing what else to do, I dragged the girls, ages seven and ten at the time, back into school where we bumped into the head of upper school – a.k.a. my boss.

He must have read the fury on my face. "Is everything OK?"

"Yeah, I just can't get my car out."

"At least she stopped swearing," Rachel blurted. She looked directly at my supervisor who held onto his concerned look. He didn't seem surprised by her comment, but he didn't laugh either.

Curse words relieved my tension surrounding Sonia's emergency as well. I couldn't imagine what news Sonia would share with me. Her insistence on speaking to me in person as soon as possible convinced me it was important. Sonia was no drama queen. We had developed a solid friendship, and she was not afraid to ask me for favors when she was truly in need. But she was careful not to impose too much, though I never minded helping her. So I wondered, what could it be that had me speeding to Providence on this late spring afternoon?

When I finally reached the city, I slowed as I passed through the downtown area and was relieved to finally be nearing her exit. Frustration repossessed me when a series of lights and bumper-to-bumper traffic halted my progress. On the main street through her neighborhood, I sped up to avoid having to stop at another red light, unintentionally passing a school bus that had stopped to unload passengers (which later resulted in a two hundred dollar fine and a few more curse words).

I wiped the sweaty bangs from my forehead as I walked up to her apartment and rang the doorbell. Sonia stepped outside to speak to me. Her petite body looked fragile against the backdrop of rusted wire fences, discarded beer bottles and concrete lots. Her brows were wrinkled with tension, and she looked like she might erupt into tears. Although she was no longer a teenager, her scared expression and wilting posture gave her a childlike appearance. Moments passed while she mustered the nerve to spit out the words.

"I'm pregnant," she said.

Her words hung in the air as I tried to assemble my own into a coherent sound that would comfort my friend.

"All right." I swallowed hard as I tried to process the news.

I shouldn't have been shocked. Sonia had been in the U.S. for almost two years, and she and Robert had been together for most of that time. Still, I felt the earth shifting below us, and I wondered how we were going to regain our footing. I desperately wanted to wipe away the fear and shame painted all over Sonia's face.

"I did a bad thing. I feel so stupid," she said.

"Everything is going to be OK, Sonia." I wrapped my arms around her. "I know it doesn't seem like it now, but I promise you that everything will work out. Have you told Robert?"

"Yes, he wants to get married, but I don't know. I'm not ready to be a mother."

"What do *you* want to do, Sonia?"

"I'm not sure."

I sensed that Sonia felt trapped, as if her world were suddenly closing in on her like the tide. Powerless to change the situation, I struggled to find more words to comfort her, give her some direction.

"Do you love Robert?" I asked.

"Yes. I love Robert." She looked me in the eye.

I was glad to hear her say the words out loud, and I believed her.

"You need to talk to Robert about how you're feeling, Sonia," I said. "He'll understand. It's important that you work things out together."

Sonia sighed. "You're right, I guess."

"You guess?" I chuckled. "Sonia, you would be a wonderful mother. I really mean that." I wanted to make sure she knew what I knew: that she was strong and capable. Although young, Sonia had endured a lifetime of hardships. Despite her fragile appearance, Sonia was resilient and brave. It would only be a matter of time before she knew this too. I hugged her and promised I would talk to her soon.

On the way home I thought about how I might have prevented this from happening, and I privately blamed myself for her distress over a situation that should have been a source of joy. After all, Sonia didn't have a mother to guide her, and I could have stepped into the role more forcibly. All those conversations I wasn't yet ready to have with my own daughters – well, they were conversations I should've had with Sonia. Instead I had convinced myself there was no reason to meddle. Although Robert had been a steady presence in Sonia's home, they didn't act like a couple. They never exchanged a hug or kiss in front of me, not even a loving glance for that matter. Still, how could I have been so naïve?

Looking back, it makes perfect sense that I'd blame myself. I spent so much energy trying to control fate's fickle mood, I almost convinced myself I could.

14

Worlds Collide

"I was feeling tired. The graduation was kind of fancy and a little boring." -Sonia

Many rituals round out the end of a school year, and each one nudges me one step closer to summer vacation. As I stand on the front end of two unstructured months, I consider the possibilities – all the gratifying ways I could fill my time. These thoughts usually drain the tension from my body, lift my spirits. But this spring was different.

A week earlier I had finished my second triathlon. I was as fit as ever. But it was impossible to prize my good health when I really wanted to gift-wrap it, top it with a bow, and give it to Mom.

I was also carrying the recent news of Sonia's pregnancy. The knowledge had been living with me a week and I was still muddling through it, trying to picture how everything was going to work out for my friend. No amount of cleaning, planning or organizing could restore the feeling of control I had before Mom's illness and Sonia's pregnancy.

There was no imagining how off-course Sonia felt.

I tried to push the thoughts aside and focus on the happy occasion in front of me – another Moses Brown graduation. Rain hustled everyone into the field house on the north side of campus. Faculty gathered in the hallway, lined up in order of seniority. We marched into the field house and paraded through two walls of applauding seniors, as formally dressed as I'd seen them. In that moment I felt a tad famous – like when I flew from Baltimore with my one carry-on.

Speeches, handing out of diplomas, and a song filled out the ceremony. When it was over, the faculty formed two rows and applauded the graduates passing through, hugging those they were close to. Families, graduates, alumni and faculty milled around, bidding farewells, expressing gratitude, snapping photos. Most were too distracted to eat from the buffet table overspread with sandwiches, salads and brownies.

I loved my students and hated saying "good-bye." Although some of them would come back to visit, they'd be different people – older, wiser, more experienced. I enjoyed learning of their accomplishments and experiences when they returned, but I knew that on this day, I was saying "good-bye" to the people they were *now*, the ones I'd spent five days a week growing fond of. I had mixed feelings, and my gut reaction was to flee the scene as soon as possible. But I forced myself to stay for at least a half hour in case someone was looking for me, or if there was someone I didn't want to miss.

This year that person was Kyle, Eugene's first tutor. Kyle was curious about Eugene, and I updated him. After talking with Kyle, I began to make my way through the crowd when I heard familiar voices. It was Robert's sisters, Chantal and Annet. Chantal's personality – as colorful as her African dress – was always on display. She was bubbly and sarcastic, while Annet had a dry, clever sense of humor – the kind you had to pay close attention to lest you miss something hilarious. The women were a stark and almost comical contrast to my understated friend, Sonia, who I spotted a few yards away, standing next to Robert. Although it made perfect sense that they'd be here for Chantal's graduation, I was surprised to see my two worlds intersect. I had planned to visit Sonia after graduation, and seeing her here never occurred to me. For a math teacher, I wasn't very good at putting two and two together.

I called Sonia over to introduce her to my friend, Joyce, the Moses Brown athletic trainer (and my junk-food eating marathon buddy). Chantal and Annet soon breezed into our friendly circle.

"This is my sister, but you probably thought she was my mother, right?" Chantal said to Joyce.

"You're not going to miss *her*, are you?" Annet quipped.

"I tell you what I'm gonna miss. I'm gonna miss the *food* at these events," Chantal said.

"Yes," her sister agreed, "We will definitely miss the good food."

I walked out with my friends and confirmed with Sonia that I'd meet her after graduation as planned. "Yes, I'll be home," she assured.

When I arrived at Sonia's house twenty minutes later, she and Robert were sitting on opposite ends of the living room, still in their formal outfits. I sat next to Sonia. She looked up to meet my gaze for a moment, then dropped her eyes to the floor. The smile I saw on her face a half hour earlier must have left in a hurry. We sat for several moments while the silence grew loud. Robert was the first one to bring up the baby.

"We can get married," he said. "Sonia and Eugene can move in with me. I have a nice apartment near CCRI (Community College of Rhode Island)."

"Sonia is concerned about her education," I said on her behalf. "You'll help her so she can go back to school, right?" The words came out slowly and deliberately, like I had rehearsed them. I felt it was important for Sonia to hear Robert's response because these were *her* concerns.

"Yes, of course. Annet and Chantal can help take care of the baby, too. We'll figure it out together." We looked at Sonia who was still looking at the floor.

I guessed that Sonia was having difficulty imagining how all the pieces of the puzzle were going to fit – taking care of a baby, going to school, working outside the home. With her arms folded neatly around her small frame, Sonia looked like a child herself in that moment.

Robert sat perfectly composed, leaning slightly forward with his eyes on Sonia. He looked like the pillar of courage in this relationship, like someone Sonia could depend on. But

I knew that, despite their contrasting outward appearances, *both* of these young people had been doused with strength from having survived their pasts.

"Sonia doesn't like to talk about it," Robert apologized.

"I know. She's scared." I wanted so badly to take Sonia's fear and shame away, and to make everything better for her, *everything*.

"Yes, I know. We didn't plan this, but we can make it work," he said.

And I believed him. I knew that, over time, Sonia would believe him, too.

15

———

Engagement Party

"I was nervous. I thought that maybe Eugene was going to say something bad. I couldn't wait until it was over, and I could go back to my house." -Sonia

I had cleared my mind of fixed notions of engagement and marriage rituals and found myself happily without motive on the day of Sonia's engagement party. My emotions were curiosity and excitement mixed with a dash of anxiety over the timing of our arrival.

"What time is the party?" I asked Sonia days before.

"I don't know. Two o'clock?"

"Two o'clock? Is that African time, Sonia, or is that the actual time you want us to show up?"

Sonia giggled. "Come at four."

"Should I go to Annet and Chantal's house or your house?"

"Come here, maybe. To pick up Eugene and take him with you."

"I'll be at your house at four, maybe a few minutes earlier." Repeating my intentions made me feel better, as if it solidified her otherwise loose timetable.

The way Sonia and Eugene regarded time eluded me. In one way, I got the sense that time was less rigid to them, less constraining. Yet, if I was even five minutes late to Sonia's house on a routine visit, she'd say, "I thought you weren't coming." (I have never stood her up.) I was afraid that we'd arrive early or late, neither of which were acceptable on this momentous occasion.

At Sonia's house, Annet, dressed in navy sweatpants, was standing in front of the stove stirring enormous pots of food. The air was rich with aromas of brown rice and chicken. Sonia slinked out of her room dressed in an elegant golden brown dress of silky fabric that clung to her in all the right places.

I hugged her. "How are you?" I asked with a hint of drama in my voice.

"I'm fine," she said. Her enthusiasm didn't match mine. Not even a fake smile crossed her face.

"Doesn't she look beautiful?" Annet said. She looked up briefly but continued stirring.

"Yes. You look beautiful, Sonia. I love your dress." Exaggerated joy was my attempt to make everything right, to make Sonia happy at her engagement party – as if I could control such things.

I imagined Sonia wasn't looking forward to being the center of attention, but I was happy for her, happy with the direction her life was heading. Robert was a good man. His family was his first priority, and I knew he'd be a supportive husband and father. He was ambitious, as were his siblings. One brother studied at Princeton, another at Rhode Island College. Robert, himself, was on track to earn his bachelor's degree in social work in a couple years. Yes, Sonia was in good hands and there was reason to celebrate.

Those were my thoughts as I looked at Sonia, looking as beautiful as I had ever seen her, albeit not as happy. She and Robert loved each other, that much I knew. And I was pretty sure Sonia was wishing she could fast-forward past the formalities. She'd be happy once they were over.

My attention shifted to Eugene when he stepped into the living room, dressed in a charcoal suit and shiny black shoes. I wondered what emotions he was processing on this day that would alter his life as well.

Rachel and Sydney's jaws dropped at the sight of him.

"Wow," Rachel said, "Eugene, you look sharp!" He held back a smile that really wanted to show itself.

"Oh, you look like a movie star, Eugene," Annet said, making Sonia's expression soften. The shift in attention took the pressure off her for a moment. While the mood was light, I nudged Eugene and my family to the car.

It took us less than ten minutes to get to Annet and Chantal's house. Cars lined both sides of their narrow street, and rain forced streams of water down the gutter forming pond-size puddles in the road.

A white party tent covered the small yard. Eight rectangular tables for guests and two tables, perpendicular to the rest, covered with crowd-size portions of fish, rice, fried potatoes and vegetables, occupied the sheltered space.

At one end of a food table, Chantal stood with some of her friends from Moses Brown. The party was also for her – to celebrate her graduation. One of Chantal's closest friends, a charming young woman with tawny gold hair and soft features, was a student of mine. She lived in one of the elegant homes on the east side of Providence. Her father was a cardiologist, her mother a lawyer. Despite their clashing backgrounds, the two girls had developed a genuine friendship. It pleased me to see them huddled together, as if there weren't an ocean of differences between them.

Wayne, the girls and I sat with four men from Rwanda, all in their twenties and thirties. Poised and passionate, they spoke with Wayne about politics, education and the economy. They seemed pleased to have found a kindred spirit in my husband who could talk about current events in any corner of the world.

Their discussion was in high gear when an older gentleman stood up, adjusted his shirt, and waited for the chatter to fade. The family friend, chosen by Annet to speak on the family's behalf, explained the purpose of the celebration and bestowed blessings, first in Kinyarwanda, then in English.

As he spoke in his native tongue, I scanned the collage of faces with many shades of brown. All but a few of us white-skinned guests (including the pastor of their church, Chantal's friends from Moses Brown, my family and me) could understand the meaning of the words spoken in the Rwandan language. Yet we were all there because our lives had become intertwined with this family whose culture and background were vastly different from our own. This realization made me feel honored and grateful.

Robert spoke next. Switching between two languages, Robert announced his intent to marry Sonia, but he spoke of her without mentioning her name, as if the identity of his future wife was a secret.

"I wonder who he's talking about," Chantal commented sarcastically only loud enough for a few to hear. Once her name was revealed, Sonia stood and dragged herself to his side without looking at the guests. I didn't hear what Robert said next because I was focused on Sonia – her slight body next to Robert's solid frame, her sad eyes, her absent smile. She wanted to be anywhere else at that moment, and she didn't try to hide her feelings. No one seemed surprised, though. Clearly, her new family knew her as well as I did; no one was expecting a performance from Sonia.

When Robert was finished, it was time to eat. And eat we did! Annet's rice was my favorite. With just the right amount of seasoning, it was never too sticky or soft – unlike my rice, which had more of an oatmeal consistency.

I came from a long line of dessert people. In my family, one could never go wrong with adding another dessert to the mix. But there was no dessert table here. Perhaps it was inside? I wondered what to do with my measly pie, which would be out of place on this table of savory dishes in giant foil pans.

I later learned that dessert was not part of the traditional

Rwandan meal. If anything, they served fresh fruit. Annet took my pie as a gift, and Sonia later told me that the family devoured it the same evening.

The dinner chatter subsided when Robert stood to face his guests, and invited them to speak. A few rose from their seats to congratulate the young couple and wish them well. The fourth person to speak was Wayne.

"Although it's raining," he began, "today is a beautiful day. I've known Eugene and Sonia for a long time now, and we're so proud of what they've accomplished. Sonia is marrying into this wonderful family, and we couldn't be happier for her. So congratulations to you both, and may you have a long and happy life together."

With wide eyes and locked lips, Rachel and Sydney swallowed their laughter. And I imagine others did as well because, in Rwanda, rain on the day of an engagement party signals good fortune.

I was disappointed that Sonia had gone inside and missed Wayne's words. I dashed through the rain to tell her.

"He said that?" Chantal said. "I missed it!"

"Really? That's so nice," Sonia said. A trace of joy had crept back into her voice. She was relaxed now that the rituals were over. "You didn't tell Wayne about the baby, did you?"

"No. I didn't tell him. But he would understand, Sonia. He wouldn't judge you."

"Maybe. But don't tell him yet, OK?"

"OK," I promised. If this was all I could do to help Sonia, at least it was something.

16

Lives Rearranging

"Eugene was my brother, and I was not going to leave him."
-Sonia

Shortly after the engagement party, Wayne and I helped Sonia and Eugene move for the third time. Their new home was Robert's two-bedroom apartment three miles away. A plush brown sofa, covered with an assortment of pillows, and a humongous flat-screen TV filled the living space. A large, shiny print of a young couple – with the woman carrying a baby on her back – hung on the wall behind the sofa. The living area extended to a narrow kitchen with a small table that defined the dining area.

Since he had no income of his own, Eugene had no choice but to move with his sister. The space was tight for three adults and a baby, but Eugene was fortunate that Robert and

Sonia were willing to support him – at least until he graduated from high school.

Despite Sonia's dedication to her brother, their relationship
remained strained. When I asked her what Eugene thought
about being an uncle, Sonia confessed, "I don't know. I
haven't said anything to him about it." I was stunned, but she
assured me that he knew about the baby without her saying
the words.

Eugene was unusually withdrawn on moving day. For the
two years they had lived in the United States, the only family
Eugene and Sonia had had was each other. Now that his sister
was engaged to Robert, Eugene's world was being rearranged
like furniture and there was nothing he could do about it.

I stepped into his room and looked for something easy to
lug to the car. One picture hung on his wall. It was the photo
of all of us at the beach their first summer in the U.S. I had
given it to him for Christmas. The blue framed five-by-seven
photo looked lonely on the bare off-white wall.

Half-packed items and dust balls littered the floor. An army
of shoes lined the wall – man-sized, unsoiled black and white
basketball sneakers with various accent colors, maybe fifteen
pairs. Although I had assumed a maternal role with Eugene,
it was not my place to ask him why he needed so many shoes
or whether he bought them before or after he lost his job. I
was there to help him move.

We loaded the car with his remaining possessions and
made the short trip to Robert's house. Only a couple trips up
the two flights of stairs and he was completely settled in his
new space. Then, with bowed head, Eugene requested we

drop him off at his old apartment so he could spend the night there.

"Really? But you don't have anything there, not even a bed," I said.

"Yes," he murmured, leaving us no choice.

I couldn't help but worry as we drove home, leaving Eugene in his barren apartment.

In the following weeks, Eugene poured his energy and attention into his schoolwork. According to Sonia, he barely spoke to her or Robert. He came home, shut himself in his bedroom and emerged briefly for the dinner Sonia prepared.

"He doesn't clean up, cook, do laundry, nothing," Sonia complained to me one day. "He can't even say 'hello' or 'good-bye,' just walks out the door like a stranger."

I figured that a summer job for Eugene would fix at least a couple of the siblings' problems. Money for Eugene and space for Sonia were not the least of them. But how motivated was he to find a job? Eugene declared education a top priority with his every move. Less clear was where he placed other goals, like earning money.

Eugene was making regular visits to the International Institute, and I was heartened by his effort but not convinced anyone would help him. The employees were busy finding jobs, securing apartments and arranging classes for new arrivals. Eugene had been in the U.S. for two years and could fend for himself.

What I didn't realize was that Eugene had made a connection with a new employee at the International Institute. Her name was Sarah. She was a job developer but not assigned to work with high-school students. Nevertheless, she was someone who had developed affection for Eugene and was willing to go out of her way to help him. She had been to the new apartment. I was happy when I learned of this new friendship, happy to know Eugene had another advocate – someone who was accessible to him.

It was early May when Eugene hit me over the head with news of a summer job opportunity on Block Island, working at a hotel. We were sitting on his sofa, TV blasting. Sonia was cooking. Smells of onions and fried potatoes infused the room and warmed the space. I took off my sweater.

"I love Block Island!" I spouted. "It would be perfect, Eugene! You love the beach!" Yes, I wanted what was best for Eugene. But hindsight convinces me that my own teenage dream had more to do with my reaction to his news than anything else.

My friend, Laura, and I had planned to spend the summer after our junior year in college working on Cape Cod. I'd take any job, live under any conditions, to realize that dream. For a variety of reasons (the main one being the boyfriend in medical school), my plan never materialized. I had often wondered if I had made the right choice. My younger self couldn't imagine that I'd ever again have the opportunity to be near sand and sea for three months.

Eugene's expression didn't mirror my excitement.

"I don't know," he mumbled, staring at the TV commercial. A siren's wail grew loud in the background.

"What do you mean? Why wouldn't you want this job?"

His words grazed my nerves as if I were having a conversation with my own teenager.

"I would have to cook," he said, still looking away.

"What?" A small gasp escaped me.

I could see Sonia chuckling, as if she had heard this saga before.

"Well, I think it would be a big mistake not to go for it, Eugene. You'd be near the beach, making money, and it would look great on your college application," I said as convincingly as I could. His cutting look inspired a more compassionate approach. "I know it's scary being on your own," I started to say.

"I'm not scared!" Eugene interrupted. He shot me a look that would send Mother Theresa running for cover. Sonia laughed, and the siren faded into the distance.

"OK," I said apologetically, sensing I had said enough – for now.

A few days later, when Sonia and I were alone, she asked me if I could be the parent and *make* Eugene take the job.

"He's never had a parent to make him do anything," she said, hands on hips.

"I can't make him do anything, Sonia," I replied. "But *you* can." She didn't like that response. I explained that she was the only one in a position to influence Eugene. He was completely dependent on her, and she asked for nothing in return. He didn't cook, clean or do laundry. He wasn't even friendly.

"Sonia, it's up to you. It's your house, and you can make the rules." Her expression suggested she didn't *feel* in control of Eugene. Sonia's empathy for her brother, which she held alongside her irritation, complicated the situation. She was, after all, the only one who really knew what her brother had been through, what he had seen. She didn't think she could bring herself to take a firm stand with him, but we were both to find out that she was wrong.

Two weeks later, same time, same place, Eugene smashed our hopes with the news that he was not taking the job on Block Island.

I was reluctant to help him find another job. I wanted him to jumpstart his own life. But I feared if I backed off, he might loaf around the apartment all summer.

And he did.

He slept long hours and kept mostly to himself, locked up in his room. Whenever I visited, I'd joke about his behavior. "He's sleeping, really? In the middle of the afternoon?" I'd speak in a deliberately loud voice. Then I'd tell Sonia to wake him up, make him come out and talk to us.

Sonia's agitation with him was piling up. I was concerned he might be depressed.

"He doesn't talk to anybody or do anything," Sonia complained to me one afternoon. "He just goes to his room and that's it, closes his door."

I bit my tongue. I had felt for a while that Sonia was spoiling Eugene, but I was in no position to judge. He was the only family she had, and she was mighty protective of him. It was easy for me to tell her she should take a firm stand with Eugene, make him step up and do his part. But the situation was dicey. I didn't know what I would've done if I were in her shoes. The truth was, I wasn't feeling confident in my ability to help *anyone*. It seemed that every time Eugene and Sonia really needed my help, I failed them. I couldn't get Eugene a computer or a new ESL teacher, and I wasn't able to take away Sonia's fears about being a mother. So much for my original plan!

And then there was Mom.

17

Mom's Courage

Although I was sorry I wouldn't be spending much time with Eugene and Sonia, I looked forward to our first full summer on Cape Cod. Sonia could've guilted me for taking off to my summer home while she endured the inland humidity and remained relatively confined to her third-floor air-conditioned apartment, with her brother sleeping most of the day, but she didn't. She often asked how I was doing and said she hoped I was having fun at the Cape, with never a hint of envy.

A summer of uninterrupted days where I could decide what to do in the moment was a gift I planned to savor. The self-containment of the Cape made it its own little world, separate and distinct from the hustle and bustle of the neighboring towns on the other side of the bridge. The culture of the Cape was one that was shaped by the sea. Conversations and news revolved around the tides, seals, and clams – and an occasional shark sighting.

There were few people I knew who loved the Cape as much as I did. Mom was one of them. The three days she spent with us on the Cape the summer of 2010 included some of my favorite moments with her.

It was late August, the peak of tourist season. The mornings were cool, but the bright sun assured another perfect beach day on the horizon. Off Cape, the air was too thick to breathe, but the Cape's ocean breeze tempered the heat's sting, and made it bearable to be outdoors even in the middle of the afternoon when the sun was perched high in the sky.

My parents arrived on a Thursday morning. Wayne was working in Rhode Island and planned to join us that evening. Mom, Dad, the girls and I spent the morning at a nearby bayside beach. It was low tide, and the color of the aquamarine sky reflected in the shallow water. The sand glistened with pink and purple hues.

Cape Cod has the distinct shape of a bent arm, with Brewster in the crease – opposite the elbow. On a clear day, the tip of the Cape was visible from our Brewster beach. When the tide was at its farthest point, you'd think you could walk straight to P-town and touch the peninsula's tip like a pencil.

Mom and I walked from sand bar to sand bar, crossing tidal pools, looking for shells and hermit crabs. Mom wore a floppy white hat and loose swim cover, faded from years of use. Our eyes fastened to the ocean floor like we were in a trance – hypnotized by the simple pleasure of treasure hunting. Occasionally one of us would look up, hold out a stone or shell for approval. "Oh, that's a good one," we'd say to validate each other's keen eye. We could have done this for hours, but the girls wanted to go swimming.

Although the beach was most picturesque during low tide, it was nearly impossible to swim then unless you were willing to trek out a couple miles to reach waist deep water. We opted to go to Flax Pond.

Flax Pond was one of the eight freshwater ponds within the wooded confines of Nickerson State Park. After spending a day earlier in the summer exploring and rating each pond in Brewster, the girls decided Flax was their favorite. Crystal-clear water devoid of weeds and muck was key to its high rating. It got crowded, but only in mid-afternoons during the popular vacation months of July and August. Hordes of tourists packed the small beach on this hot day, but we were committed.

We dropped our bags and set up our chairs in the middle of the beach. Woodlands shaded the edge of the waterfront, creating prime real estate for beach dwellers on a scorching day. We hadn't brought our umbrella, so the water looked especially inviting. Dad was the only one who could resist its allure. Despite the intense heat of the day, Dad relaxed in his chair with a content look on his face.

"Make sure you put sunscreen on, Joe," Mom insisted.

"Yeah, Dad," I said, "Be careful of your ankles. Remember what happened to your ankles?"

Dad laughed. Of course he remembered because it happened every year. He'd wear socks all summer except when vacationing at the Cape. While he was lying on the beach, the sun would roast his virgin skin, turning his ankles and feet blistery red. He looked like he had painted on his socks.

I tossed Dad the lotion with the highest SPF and headed down to the water with Mom. The girls had already plunged in.

Rachel and Sydney amused each other on the opposite side of the swimming area. Surrounded by vacationers, Mom and I felt like we were alone in our Cape Cod pond, like we were *at home*. We leaned back, dunked our heads and let the water cradle us. A blissful expression covered Mom's face as she let the cool water soothe her body, while the sun pressed against her face.

"I could die now and I would die happy," she said. I didn't feel the need to respond. I knew what she meant, and she knew I knew. We shared a deep love for this place, and we were both grateful to be here together. I felt completely *present*.

That evening was filled with Cape Cod traditions. We grilled fresh seafood and made a salad from our garden vegetables. After dinner, we settled our stomachs with a walk to the ice cream shop a mile away. Mom got maple walnut, Dad chose black raspberry. Then we hiked a bit further to watch the sunset over the sea's horizon. The sunsets over the bay were spectacular and ever changing. Fiery reds, yellows and oranges melted into pinks and purples that reflected themselves in the shimmering water. We stood silently, mesmerized by nature's grand performance.

This is how we'd spend many evenings, but these would be the last to include Mom.

Rachel and Sydney were both attending a day camp three days a week, Sydney as a camper and Rachel as a counselor in training. This gave me the opportunity to spend the following day alone with Mom while Wayne took Dad out on the boat we had recently acquired from Wayne's mother.

After dropping off the girls at Brewster Day Camp, a rustic camp tucked in the woods abutting Nickerson State Park, Mom and I continued down route 6A heading east. We eventually landed in downtown Wellfleet, a quaint seaside town adorned with souvenir shops, art galleries and unique restaurants. Mom and I strolled here and there, ducking into shops that captured our fancy. My favorite one, a lavender building with a pointy roof, housed local hand-crafted jewelry. Mom was determined to get something for the girls and me, but we'd have to wait until Christmas to enjoy our gifts. The earrings I picked out were shaped like toothpicks, but they dangled and were a brilliant gold. The ones we agreed on for Rachel were blue-green like the ocean. For Sydney, we found a mug with a ceramic dog glued inside. Perfect.

The next shop that grabbed our attention was a periwinkle one with cream trim and a bountiful flower garden in front. Mom was looking for a more attractive summer hat to shade her hairless head. She tried on several at the back of the store until she found one we both agreed was most flattering. White with blue trim and a narrow rim, it fit Mom's head like it was made for her.

Mom knew I had recently lost my sunglasses, and she

insisted on buying me a new pair. After trying on several, I found a pair that didn't make me look like a bug. They were rosy brown with rhinestones on the sides. When the sunglasses broke a few days later, I cried – not because they were expensive or all that attractive, but because there wouldn't be many more gifts from Mom. This made them suddenly invaluable.

When we tired of shopping, we drove down to the harbor for lunch. Before eating, we poked into one more store, which sold paintings by local artists.

"Your work is so much better," Mom whispered as we meandered through the two small rooms. This was something only a mother would say and actually mean. Although I knew it wasn't true, I loved that Mom thought it was.

The smell of fried seafood wafted from the pier and magnified our hunger as we approached the ocean-side clam shack. We each ordered an over-stuffed lobster roll and Diet Coke. While we sat at the picnic table savoring our fresh seafood, we took in the panoramic view of the ocean, along with its salty smells. Seagulls trumpeted a loud melody over our heads as the sea's distant roar hummed in the background. Few words passed between us. We were in heaven after all, and conversation was unnecessary.

A stretch of land shaped like my mixed collie's tail jutted into the bay across the harbor. "I wonder how you get over *there*," I thought out loud, as a spirited breeze tried to snatch my napkin.

Mom and I shared an adventurous spirit. Today our mission was to get to the peninsula we had admired many times

157

like a favorite photograph. Mom loved maps. She loved reading them, trying to find the best way to get someplace. So off we went. I drove, Mom navigated. We made several turns down winding roads and eventually came upon a pencil-thin street brushed with beach sand. It led to a small lot. We passed maybe three cars. I was always surprised by how easy it was to escape tourists on the Cape, even during high season.

The view captivated us as soon as we stepped away from the car. We hiked to the stretch of land we had been eying from afar and looked across the water back toward the clam shack. Brush and dunes lined the center of the jutting earth, encouraging us to walk to the tip for simultaneous views of the shore and open sea. A narrow beach skimmed both sides of the peninsula. An empty bench and a woman checking oyster traps were the only hints of human life on our side; the other was dotted with a handful of sunbathers. I slowed my thoughts so I could appreciate this time with Mom, with the full knowledge that these moments would soon be a bittersweet memory.

The Brew Run came on my parents' last day on the Cape. Each year, Brewster attracted over a thousand people to the five-mile race, which started and ended at the Woodshed, a small local bar that remained a well-kept secret from tourists. I wasn't sure if it was called the Brew Run because it took place in Brewster or because they gave free beer to finishers – perhaps both. In any case, I had registered months ago and was excited to participate, not because of the free beer, but because my family could watch me from the end of our street.

Mom never understood why I ran. I imagined she thought it was a form of self-inflicted torture resulting from a personality disorder. Why else would someone get up before dawn to run in the dark with Vaseline on her face in sub-freezing temperatures? Or head out in the July heat, water and fuel strapped to her body, while blisters grew on her feet. And the injuries, well those could be avoided by simply not running.

Mom couldn't fathom the satisfaction and excitement that running brought me. The training provided me with time alone on a regular basis, and increased my physical strength while quelling my anxiety. (Can you imagine me *without* exercise?) It forced me outdoors, into nature's arms, and gave me an outlook adjustment. The races motivated me. They were the culmination of the hard work I had done, a celebration of what I'd already accomplished. There was no way she could possibly understand without witnessing it firsthand.

Although I had run three marathons, completed three triathlons and participated in countless shorter races, Mom had never seen me run. I'd always secretly wanted her to, but I never told her. I felt my mother should just know what was important to me and was disappointed that she didn't. It made no sense, really. I just accepted that Mom was never going to visit that part of my life, and she hadn't. Until now.

At 3:15, I rode my bike to the Woodshed, checked in at the registration table, did some stretches and headed for the start. As the crowd closed in around me, I tried to take it all in – the coconut scent of suntan lotion, the small-town charm, and the upbeat tempo of the Zach Brown Band coming through my MP3 player. Then the gun sounded and we were off.

I felt strong as I ran down the familiar roads of Brewster. The four o'clock start was an unusual time for a race, and the sun's strength was still palpable. But I was caught up in the moment, encouraged by cheering spectators and garden hoses pointed in my direction. I was feeling high, enjoying the healthy sound of my breath and the way my body seemed to move like a well-oiled machine – a result of the consistent training I had done over the previous weeks. The salt of my sweat mingled with the salt in the air and I could taste it. I thought about how fun it would be to do this race the following year with Rachel, who was just starting her running career that fall as a member of the cross-country team.

As I made my way down Tubman Road, approaching the point where it met the end of my street, I moved toward the side of the road to make myself visible to my family who would be standing there. Once I caught sight of them, I waited until I was within shouting range before I made myself heard. Not by my family, but by *her*. "Hi, Mom!" were the words that spilled out without premeditation. For a moment our eyes locked and a smile crossed her face. I wound around the next corner with a fresh spring in my step, feeling immensely gratified.

The entire year after my mother's diagnosis, I felt like I was swinging on an emotional pendulum. Exhausted physically and mentally, I had no idea that this was just the beginning. My family's highs and lows were dependent on Mom's cancer count, the intensity of the chemotherapy's side effects and our own ability to deal with the reality of her prognosis at any given moment.

The year following Mom's diagnosis could have been much worse. Despite the many hardships and disappointments, Mom's attitude never wavered. It was impossible to be morose around someone with so much spunk and optimism. Although she basically received a death sentence when she was told she had stage-four ovarian cancer, she shared few of the realities of her prognosis with me and succeeded in letting me hold on to a glimmer of hope.

That all changed the October after her diagnosis. I had just come home from school when the phone rang. Recognizing Mom's number, I grabbed the receiver. We spoke often, but Mom only called *me* when there was news to share. I wasn't expecting good news, but I also wasn't prepared for the words she spoke.

"I just saw Dr. Sparrow," Mom began. "He said I have six months to two years." Mom spoke with a staid calmness, as if telling me what she had cooked for dinner. The news shouldn't have surprised me, but it did. Suddenly cloaked in despair, I felt a huge weight overcome me. In the following months, I carried the burden with me like a backpack. Sometimes it felt less heavy, as if some of the pain had been discarded. On rare occasions, the weight was imperceptible, and I almost didn't notice how rapidly and significantly my life was changing. Other times, the weight was unbearable, and I felt lucky to merely survive the day.

The one reliable bright spot of each evening was calling Mom. She always answered the phone the same way.

"Hi, Sweetie, how are ya?" Her voice would get higher as she drew out the word "are," sounding equally delighted and surprised that I had called. I cherished hearing those words once I knew they were in short supply. I would share with Mom the details of my day, focusing on Rachel and Sydney. Mom and Dad were the only ones I could talk to freely about my daughters without feeling like a bragging parent, and Mom always reacted with the expected measure of enthusiasm and pride.

As much as I cherished those conversations, they were strikingly ordinary. Mom had a way of changing her tone or becoming suddenly quiet when I said something she didn't approve of or agree with. While the rest of the world knew her as a straight shooter, she had a much more subtle and often confusing way of communicating with me. I never called her on it, and maybe that was a mistake. Instead, I would analyze the meaning behind her mysterious inflections and pauses. This dynamic didn't change when Mom got sick. What changed was the pile of guilt that came afterwards. One time Wayne found me in my bedroom crying after speaking with Mom on the phone.

"Are you sad about your mother?" he asked, trying to show support.

"Yes," I answered. "But it's not what you think."

"What is it?"

"I feel guilty because she can still make me mad!"

Mom started a new type of chemotherapy that week, and it happened to be on a day I didn't have classes. Seniors were off campus visiting colleges, sophomores and juniors would be taking PSATs, and freshmen were going on a field trip. So I joined Mom and Dad.

The morning of the treatment, I arrived at my parents' house at 8:00 am. Mom, as usual, was a bundle of good cheer. She joked about how patient my dad had been with her when they went shopping in Boston a week earlier. "He felt bad for me because I have cancer," she said, grinning.

At the clinic, Mom's doctor explained how the new chemotherapy worked. The good news was that it would take a fraction of the time her previous therapy took, giving us time to spend elsewhere.

After speaking with the doctor, we moved to a large, open room, with patients seated on the perimeter, each getting their allotted dose of cancer medicine.

"You're back again?" one receptionist said to Mom with a sympathetic tone.

"Yup," she said. "This time we're really going to get it!" Mom waved her fist in the air.

I sat next to her as a nurse injected her with needles. Mom sweetly, but firmly, demanded to know everything that was happening and why. The nurse kindly answered all her questions.

The side effects would kick in after a few days. Mom scheduled her treatment so she'd be sick on the weekends and feel better during the week so she could work. She insisted on working as long as she was able. When she was too weak to drive to work, she did what she could from home – but she never stopped.

Mom felt better as her treatment neared. If I was able to time my visits right, life was good. This day was a bonus. The new treatment took only a couple hours, and Mom had energy and appetite. So we went out for lunch. We ate, talked and laughed – as if everything was right in our world.

18

Sonia's Shower

"I didn't know it was going to happen. Usually the mother plans the shower, or the sisters. I didn't have a mother or sisters." -Sonia

Sonia grew increasingly tired as her body adjusted to the new life inside her belly. Her small frame looked like it was carrying an oversized watermelon on its front side. I gave Sonia a copy of *What to Expect When You're Expecting* and shared with her my pregnancy anecdotes to assure her that her peculiar and sometimes embarrassing symptoms were perfectly normal. Sonia had a tendency to worry now that she was nearing motherhood. Her maternal instincts were strong.

A more content Sonia was going through the nesting phase, dutifully organizing her space to make room for the baby and preoccupied with acquiring the necessary items before its arrival. I promised to take her shopping for baby supplies, and this comforted her. If anyone understood the calming effect of thoughtful preparation, it was me. How could I deprive my dear friend of this remedy?

Two days after my promise to Sonia, Chantal called to invite me to Sonia's baby shower.

"Oh, no! I promised to take Sonia baby shopping," I said once I realized who I was speaking to. I had never heard Chantal's phone voice, and she didn't identify herself.

"Oh well, you will just have to suddenly get sick. Yes, you will be sick," Chantal instructed.

"But she'll be so upset," I whined.

"That's fine." Chantal didn't care. She wouldn't have to hear Sonia's sorrow.

I thought about cancelling long enough to imagine Sonia's disappointment, my anxiety and guilt. About five seconds. This shopping trip was going to happen even if I had to physically restrain Sonia from buying too many would-be shower gifts.

And so it did.

Annet asked to join us, so I picked her up after Sonia. As the three of us walked across the parking lot to the large box store, Annet told me about her brother who was still in Africa with his three children. Annet had never met her nieces and nephew. Sonia's baby would be the first one she'd know.

Sonia pulled a shopping cart from the lot and directed it into Annet's hands.

"I can push the cart," I said.

"No, she can do it. She needs to practice steering anyway. You should see how she drives," Sonia teased.

As we roamed the aisles of the infant section, Annet and I inspected the items and offered our opinions on the importance (or lack thereof) of each one. I found products I didn't recognize, and some that seemed just plain gimmicky. Humidifiers, purifiers, wipe warmers, fold-up baby nail clippers – so many decision to make. Sonia paid close attention and didn't seem to mind having two women offering her advice. Annet scrutinized each outfit in the girls' section (yes, she was having a girl), and held up the ones she considered most essential to her niece's wardrobe.

Sonia didn't buy *too* much that day: a changing pad, bottles, a thermometer, and lots of clothes. Annet could be awfully persuasive.

When we returned to Sonia's apartment, Annet and I showcased each outfit for Robert. He was a good sport, expressing his approval of each article – down to every sock and bib. Sonia watched and giggled.

The Sunday before Thanksgiving was the day of Sonia's surprise baby shower. Annet had called me a couple times about the timing, but we still managed to get our wires crossed. Panic and excitement filled the air when we arrived at Annet's house, obviously late. Anxiety took over my joyful spirit but only for a moment.

"Everyone kept saying, 'No, Chris isn't here! Chris has to be here!'" one woman said. "I was wondering who this important person was."

I was important? To Sonia? I clung to that thought for a while, easing back into my cheerful mood.

Annet greeted me with a hug. Chantal's energy infused the room like fairy dust. Family and friends gathered quietly in the living room to the right of the entranceway. Others, mostly men, gathered in the kitchen at the end of the short hallway. A multi-colored throw and pink balloons decorated a chair strategically placed so loved ones could see the guest of honor from the living room, hallway and kitchen.

Rachel and Sydney crouched by the window on the landing of the stairway where they had a clear view of the street. Their job was to warn us of Sonia and Robert's arrival.

When Rachel gave the signal, Annet and Chantal fled to the door. Dressed in a t-shirt and jeans, Chantal opened the door when Sonia, Robert, and Eugene stepped onto the front porch. Apparently she couldn't wait for them to come to the door. Covering her face with her hands, Sonia let Chantal pull her inside. A line of women waited to hug her. She was wearing loose fitting gray pants with a white shirt, covered by a tan argyle sweater. Her hair was pulled back, and her expression was one of both joy and discomfort at being the center of attention – again. It was a massive huddle, with Sonia at the center and everyone trying to get the special moment on camera. Loud voices speaking Kinyarwanda competed with one another. Dressed sharply in a white shirt and corduroy sports coat, Robert was beaming.

Sonia settled into the festive chair. She turned toward Rachel and Sydney. "Why didn't you tell me?" she playfully demanded. "And you, Chris, you didn't help me either!"

"Did Sonia suspect anything?" I heard someone ask Robert.

"She knew something was up when she saw me ironing my trousers," he said still beaming. "I never iron my clothes."

"What does the princess feel like drinking?" Annet asked, pointing to Sonia's round stomach.

"Juice would be good. Thank you," Sonia said.

As Annet scurried to the kitchen, she announced, "Well, I think we should eat, so we can go ahead and get to the point!" Chantal had already unwrapped the foil coverings of the massive pans of food and the savory smells overtook the small space, whetting an appetite I didn't know I had. As usual, the women in Robert's family outdid themselves, preparing a delicious feast of traditional African food. I stood in the narrow hallway with most of the men.

I sipped my beer and felt momentarily self-conscious for being the only woman holding a beer bottle. I wondered if I was violating some cultural rule of etiquette. I let my angst slip out, and Annet immediately set me straight.

"Oh, it's fine – we drink beer!" she said. Chantal laughed at my concern. I should've known. Even if I had misstepped, this was the most forgiving group I could've done it with.

It was the first time I had met some of Robert's brothers and their wives. One woman asked me how I knew Sonia and I reached for the right words to describe our relationship. I started as a volunteer mentor, but our relationship had outgrown that description; it didn't do justice to the friendship we had built. I think I just told her we met at the International Institute.

Eugene stood quietly in the corner as he typically did at gatherings of more than a few people. I guessed he enjoyed being pulled into this large caring family despite his detached body language.

While we ate, Chantal toted Sonia's presents in from the bedroom. She tore off the covering of each one, held the items in front of Sonia's face and provided a running commentary for everyone's amusement. This was unlike any shower I'd been to, and I was fairly certain I wasn't witnessing a traditional African shower. No, I was pretty sure this was Chantal's unique take-charge way of doing things. Sonia was center stage but the action was taking place all around her. It was like watching the Chantal show, with Annet as the supporting actress. No one seemed to mind, least of all Sonia.

Sonia received many generous gifts, including two car seats, a crib, and several handmade blankets from Annet. I bought her one of the car seats and made a baby quilt for her, but in the frenzy of gifts that were revealed, I was disappointed that mine didn't stand out more. Regardless, I was thrilled for my friend. Chantal made sure everyone had their picture taken with Sonia holding the gift they had brought. I had my moment and was happy.

As my family was saying good-bye, Chantal asked, "When are you going to have us over? How long have we known each other, and we have never been to your house?"

"You can come over anytime." I meant it, sort of. I would've loved to have Chantal and Annet over, as much as I would've loved to have anyone. They were two of the funniest people I knew. I loved the way this family had so much fun together, and I wanted to be a part of it to the extent that they'd let me. But truth be told, I was a bit of a recluse:

I rarely invited anyone over. Cooking and cleaning for company stressed me to no end. I wished it didn't, and I admired people who could entertain when their house was in disarray. I wasn't one of them and wanting to be wouldn't make it so. But how could I say, "I like you and want to be friends, but I'm a social phobic so stay away"? I don't think I could and not sound like a jerk. Full disclosure: One of my best friends at school, who I'd known for sixteen years, had never been to my house. Not kidding.

"You don't need an invitation," I said.

"What are you doing on Thanksgiving?" Chantal asked. "We'll come then." We were almost all the way out the door at this point, so I just glanced in her direction as I continued my forward motion.

"We won't be home on Thanksgiving," I finally said. With that, we bolted.

On the car ride home, Wayne and I shared conversations we'd had with Robert's family.

Eugene had updated Wayne on Jean Pierre. After graduation, Jean Pierre had moved to North Carolina with three thousand dollars in his pocket. It was money he had convinced his parents he needed for the school he'd be attending, and they never questioned him. But he never went to school. He spent the money and took odd jobs to make ends meet. Eugene didn't seem interested in Jean Pierre anymore. Maybe he lost respect for him. In Eugene's eyes, there was nothing more important than education.

19

Eugene Lets Me In

*"Taking two French classes at the same time was crazy. And I had
to take a class at night in order to graduate." -Eugene*

After a summer devoid of responsibility, Eugene suddenly
had many demands on his time. A new superintendent had
changed the graduation requirements, with no exceptions for
seniors. Every time I saw Eugene that fall, I got a new update.
He was told he had to take evening courses to satisfy his
graduation requirements, but he wasn't sure where or when.
Then he was told he was all set. I made some phone calls
in search of answers, but landed in the same muck swamp
as Eugene. Eventually it was clear he had to take additional
classes, and I was furious that he was now getting this information when he had an entire summer in his rearview. He
even had to take an extra level of French, which meant he'd

be taking two levels simultaneously. This was beyond ridiculous, in my opinion.

In addition to taking extra courses, Eugene was focused on college applications. Two local programs, in particular, suited him. They were designed for students who had academic challenges, such as English not being their first language. The applications stated a requirement of four years of high school English, which Eugene didn't have. He had taken several ESL courses, and I cautioned him that they weren't the same. Nevertheless, he insisted on applying, and I wasn't going to be the one to stand in his way. In other words, I helped.

He was also getting help from Sarah at the International Institute, and I thought it would be a good idea if she and I were on the same page. One day after visiting Eugene, I walked over to the Institute to introduce myself to the person who had managed to earn Eugene's trust. The receptionist at the refugee resettlement office directed me to Sarah's cubicle. There were few people around at the late hour, but Sarah was still at her desk working. As soon as I introduced myself, a pleased expression flashed across her face. I learned we were the same age, but the twinkle in her eye and stylish haircut made her seem younger, more hip. I could see right away why Eugene liked her.

"He's been coming almost every day," she said. "He came in here the other day to see if I could help him with geometry. I was out sick a couple days, and he made some sarcastic comment about how I'm never here." She paused. "Yeah, there's just something about that boy. He can drive me nuts at times, but at other times he can be so sweet."

We chatted for a long time about Eugene, our experiences with him and how best to help him with his college applications. I've met few people with whom I've felt an instant connection – Sarah was one of them; it felt like we'd known each other for years.

"Did Eugene tell you how he got fired from his job?" Sarah asked and then seemed surprised that he hadn't. "He pulled the fire alarm," she told me. My jaw dropped.

"What?" I said in disbelief. "Why would he do that?"

"I don't know. I guess he just wanted to see what would happen."

According to Sarah, Eugene *did* want the Block Island job. The interview didn't go well because Eugene didn't make eye contact. (I later read that direct eye contact with superiors is considered rude in Rwandan culture.) Then he took a long time to give his decision. When he did, it was too late.

"There's something about that boy," Sarah repeated. She shook her head. "There's just something about him that makes me want to help him."

I knew exactly what she meant.

It took several visits to help Eugene complete his college applications and financial aid forms. I was worried that asking him some of the questions would make us both feel uncomfortable – questions about his parents' deaths, for example.

I sat on the sofa beside Eugene one afternoon, laptop in front of us. Sonia was in the kitchen.

He handed me his essay. When I got to the second paragraph, I made myself slow down to absorb every word. As though it were nothing, Eugene had handed me his painful past on a piece of paper. As though it were nothing, he finally exposed those dark moments of his life that I never dared to ask about.

I was born in Rwanda. I never knew my father because he died when I was young. He was Hutu. My life became hard because I was with my mother (she was Tutsi) and she had to take care of three children: my older sister, my older brother and me. My other brothers were grown and we didn't know where they were. One brother was killed as part of the genocide. He was 25 years old. I saw this and was very afraid. It was all crazy. My mother took my sister and me and fled Rwanda. We went by foot to the Congo to a refugee camp. The food was awful and I didn't feel safe. You can never feel safe if it is not your house. We went back to Rwanda where my mother died. It was not safe for my sister and me as orphans in Rwanda, and it was scary that we were 16 and 14 and could be killed. We went to Tanzania then to Zambia. Life was hard. We stayed in Zambia as refugees for four years, until we came to the United States.

I took a deep breath, let humility take hold of my soul. I felt honored that he had shared this with me. Yet I was hesitant to ask questions, afraid of making him regret his decision to let me read about his past. Besides, they were a child's memories and, as such, their details vulnerable to inaccuracy. The emotions were real, though, and that was something I wanted to protect.

I made a few comments, showed him how to attach the essay to his application, and moved on to the rest of the form.

"Your father's name?" I asked Eugene. He said something, which I didn't quite get. Sonia turned around with a *What are you saying?* look on her face. They went back and forth for a bit, arguing over their father's name and in minutes we were all laughing.

The rest of the questions were easy.

Sonia and Eugene were finally getting along. Earlier that month, Sonia had had a frank conversation with her brother about his behavior.

The next day, he vacuumed the apartment.

"Maybe I will just go in the army," Eugene said without looking up. He sounded serious, but the laughter from the kitchen told me otherwise.

"Maybe I will move away to Kentucky, start a new life."

"What are you talking about?" I wanted to see where he would take this conversation if I went along. "You can't move."

"Why not?"

"Because I would miss you."

Eugene finally picked his head up and looked at me. "I would miss you, too." He fiddled with the remote control. "But, I have to do what I need to do to have a better life."

Sonia was snickering.

"Eugene, you don't need to move to have a better life. You

need to keep going to school. You're young. You can do anything you want to do." I meant every word. "When I was your age, I had very little."

I described my first apartment in Worcester, Massachusetts. The narrow city blocks were lined with triple-decker apartment buildings, so close you could almost touch someone next door if you both leaned out your windows and stretched your arms as far as possible. Each closet-size bedroom had its own character. Mine, with its mud-colored paneling, screamed seventies. My roommate had the funky L-shaped room with the tired green shag carpet. The whole building was in complete disrepair, and the kitchen floor had such a steep grade that if you accidently dropped a pen in just the right way, it would roll clear across the room. On more than one occasion, my roommate and I found ourselves face to face with neighborhood boys standing in our living room. They had climbed through one of the bedroom windows that had a broken lock.

Eugene shot me a look of disbelief, as if he only imagined me in a nice house with a nice yard. "I rode my bike to two jobs in two different towns before I had a car. I went to school, but I also worked full time to pay my bills."

Yes, it was true that I had a family who had my back, a solid high-school education, and mastery over the English language. And my white privilege was not lost on me. I was not comparing my situation to Eugene's. My point was, everyone has to work to get what he or she wants in life, and it wouldn't happen overnight – Eugene would need to be patient with himself.

20

Charlotte

"I was so scared. I thought, 'Oh my God, I'm not going to push out the baby. How am I going to know when it's ready to come? I think I'm going to die.' When they started talking about the contractions, I had no idea what they were talking about." -Sonia

I finished writing a calculus test, replied to e-mails, and scanned the Post-its on my desk. With a half hour before my next class, I decided to check my phone messages. I felt guilty that this was the first time I was checking for a message from Sonia. It was, after all, three days past her due date, so there was no accounting for my surprise at discovering that Robert had sent me a text moments earlier telling me Sonia was in the hospital.

When I first learned of Sonia's January first due date, I was struck by the irony of it. At some point during the first months of our relationship, I had asked Eugene and Sonia when their birthdays were.

"January first," Sonia murmured, and repeated herself when I asked about Eugene's.

"Wow, you both have the same birthday!" I was amused by the unlikely coincidence. Eugene and Sonia didn't seem at all surprised, and it was a year later when I discovered why.

Many African refugees were without birth records. Only those lucky enough to be born in a hospital during a time of relative peace could be certain of their birth date. The government assigned all others the birthday of January first. I learned this from a book I read one summer about a man's journey to the United States. It was an "aha" moment for me, but one that made me feel naïve, if not stupid. Sonia's January first due date, however, was a real coincidence.

Some weeks before, Sonia had told me she wanted me with her when she gave birth. I wasn't sure if she meant by her side during delivery, or simply present at the hospital. Now I was furious with myself for not clarifying her wishes earlier. Regardless of whether or not I would be present for the birth, it was important that she knew I was close by.

I scurried to get coverage for my two remaining classes. It was a short ride to the hospital from Moses Brown, and I arrived within forty-five minutes of receiving the text.

The hospital's interior was unrecognizable from when I had birthed Sydney eleven years before. Walls must have been knocked down to make the open entranceway and large reception area, which appeared modern, futuristic even.

My first obstacle was the gray-haired receptionist peering

up from behind the large desk. No big deal. They just needed a patient's name. If only there weren't five hundred permutations of Sonia's name, all of them equally impossible to spell. I worried my hesitation would read as guilty – guilty of what, I wasn't sure. I doubted many people tried to sneak up to the maternity floor to watch strangers screaming in agony, cursing at their spouses. Luckily, after only a couple of misses, I spit out a name that came up on the computer.

"Only two people are allowed in the room at a time," the gray-haired lady informed, "and there are two people up there now." It had to be Robert and Annet. I was allowed to sit in the lobby on the first floor and, if someone came down, I could go up. I wasn't expecting to take Annet's place, but I was hoping I could go up for a minute to let Sonia know I was with her in spirit.

As I sat in the lobby, surrounded by family and friends waiting for updates on their loved ones, memories of my own childbirths rushed to mind. I remembered being startled awake in the middle of the night by the burst of amniotic fluid gushing down my legs. It was my first pregnancy. My mid-wife instructed me to eat something sweet to make sure the baby was moving and then go back to sleep. Sure, no problem, I thought, as I sat on a towel on the bathroom floor eating a granola bar, praying for movement in my belly while Wayne moved in slowly with the video camera. If I had had any energy, I might have seriously hurt him.

Of course I couldn't sleep, so we went to the hospital. There, a buxom nurse filled my veins with Pitocin, which gave marching orders to my contractions. An army of them.

And just when I was about to surrender under their onslaught, the epidural came to my rescue. I'm pretty sure it was accompanied by angels playing violins and fireworks going off. It was, after all, the fourth of July. When it was time to push Rachel out, I was completely engrossed in *General Hospital* and felt slightly bothered to have to miss the last fifteen minutes. That's how I remember the time of day my first daughter was born: It was forty-five minutes into my three o'clock soap opera.

My second birthing experience was completely different. I decided to forego the epidural and go natural because I had read it would reduce my chances of tearing. I was terrified of being ripped open, so I attended the special classes in the birthing center where they taught different methods of pain management, such as leaning against an exercise ball. If I hadn't experienced contractions before, I might have fallen for it. But, really? A bouncy ball? A man must have come up with that idea.

I kept *my* focus on the whirlpool bath. That had at least a chance in hell of comforting me during what would undoubtedly be the most painful experience of my life. And I thought about the nice room. The birthing center was like a luxurious hotel suite, and you didn't have to move out as soon as the baby came. You could sit in the living area and watch TV.

I learned a lot about myself when I gave birth to Sydney. I wasn't a screamer. I dealt with the pain of childbirth the same way I managed the pain of running a marathon: I disappeared into my head. My brain registered only necessary information from my environment, like the mid-wife telling me when to push. Everything else, like my husband's spoken encouragement, was out of my frequency range. I was distracted and focused at the same time. That quiet inner strength that I have come to rely on was passed on in spades to the daughter to whom I was giving birth.

My mind returned to Sonia when I saw Robert passing through the lobby. I caught his attention and explained what the receptionist had told me. He tried to bring me upstairs with him anyway, but we didn't get past the guard standing by the door to the stairwell.

"That's OK," I assured Robert, "Just let Sonia know I'm here."

Twenty minutes later, Chantal arrived like a rainbow. Her energy and humor hastened the hour and I was grateful. Then Robert came down again and told us we wouldn't be able to see Sonia for a while.

"Charlotte was born," he said, his face fixed in a blissful grin.

"Charlotte is here?" Chantal said. "This is good news! When can I see my niece?"

"They'll be moving Sonia to a new room, and that could take some time," Robert said. Disappointment washed over her face. I knew it was going to be a long night, but the news of Charlotte's arrival erased my exhaustion. I felt impatient, ready to see Sonia and Charlotte.

Chantal decided to go home and wait for a call. That made sense for her, because she lived nearby. And I suppose it made sense for me too, considering the wait could be hours and my drive home was only twenty-five minutes. I could go home, eat with my family and return in the evening.

Once home, restlessness and excitement overcame me, rendering me useless. I called Chantal and invited myself over. I can't remember if I grabbed something to eat on my way out. All I know is my mind was on Sonia, and I needed to do *something* if only go to the sisters' house and wait.

Chantal greeted me at the front door, and led me to the living room. A handful of friends and family filled the small living space where we practiced patience for another hour and a half. In her usual comedic fashion, Chantal kept everyone abreast of the situation while texting Annet every fifteen minutes for updates. With over a decade separating their births, I often marveled at Annet and Chantal's relationship. It seemed to flow smoothly from a sibling relationship to more of a mother-daughter relationship – no bumps in between.

A young couple I didn't recognize sat across from me. The man, dressed like he had come from a business meeting, lit up the room with his effortless smile. I imagined he had a kind heart. His casually dressed girlfriend never uttered a word or glanced in my direction. Not even Chantal could stir her. I wondered if she was tired, or carrying an invisible burden. Maybe she was comfortable enough in her skin and surroundings that she didn't feel pressed to wear a false demeanor. What would *that* be like, I wondered?

Frustrated, tired and eager to see Sonia and her baby, Chantal and I decided to head back to the hospital. There, we again waited, but only for a short time. An elated Robert greeted us and escorted us to Sonia's room.

Annet was standing beside Sonia, her expression reflecting pride and gratitude in equal measures. Sonia's eyes looked like they wanted to close, but I could tell it was a happy exhaustion. Chantal and Annet took turns holding the precious bundle that would be the new center of their world.

"I'm your favorite Auntie," Chantal said in a voice too loud for the late hour. Annet pressed her lips together in defiance as her sister continued to speak to Charlotte. I imagined how funny they'd be competing for her affection. I didn't want to be the one to break up the happy moment, but I could see Sonia had had enough for one day. I suggested we let her rest, knowing very well we'd all return the next day when Sonia would be more excited to see us.

"How was Cape Cod?" Sonia asked me when I bent over to hug her. She knew I had just returned from spending New Year's Eve there.

"What? Did you have a vacation?" Annet asked.

"We just spent a couple days on Cape Cod for New Year's Eve," I tried to deflect the attention away from myself.

"Ohhh. Cape Cod! Who are those rich people that have those big summer houses on Cape Cod?" Chantal asked.

I shrugged. I didn't have a big house, but in that moment I would've felt uncomfortable with her knowing I had any house on Cape Cod. I winked at Robert and Sonia, and slipped out of the room before the conversation could go further.

The following day, I returned to find a more vibrant Sonia. Annet was by her side, along with a woman I hadn't met before. Sonia's friend was hunched over her, helping the baby to latch onto Sonia's breast, while Annet supervised. I sat a few feet away, feeling like an intruder. Secretly I wished I was the one helping Sonia, but I knew there was no competing with these women who seemed as though they had done this a thousand times. Annet didn't have her own children, but she had watched her mother care for her younger siblings. Although I'd breastfed both my daughters, it felt like an eternity ago, and I wasn't sure I'd have the slightest idea of how to help Sonia now. Instead, I watched in admiration as these two strong, capable women supported my young friend. It took a few attempts and the wisdom of both women to get Charlotte to breastfeed.

Captivated, I barely noticed the large containers of food that lined the windowsill until Sonia's friend began uncovering layers of foil.

"Eat," she prodded, looking directly at me. Annet nodded in agreement.

"Thank you." I felt obligated to try something though I wasn't hungry. Moments later, five young men, all wearing khakis and dress shirts, filed in. After expressing their congratulations and making a few jokes amongst themselves, they happily delved into the food. I enjoyed the company I was in and would have loved to stay longer, but I had to pick up Rachel and Sydney. I said my good-byes and headed back to my car.

Robert and Eugene passed me on my way out of the parking lot. I left content with the knowledge that Eugene was about to meet his niece.

The following month, Eugene started a new job working at the Community College of Rhode Island as a janitor. Working while attending school full-time, Eugene was forging a good path for himself. I had every faith he would continue.

Like most new mothers, Sonia didn't get much sleep the first few months after Charlotte's birth. Despite the exhaustion, motherhood looked beautiful on her. The extra pounds made her appear healthier, stronger. And she was absolutely smitten with her baby. Attentive, protective, loving – she was a natural and watching her inspired me.

The nighttime feedings were nonetheless taking a toll. We talked about breast pumps. If she could pump her breast milk and save it, Robert would be able to help her with the nighttime feedings, and she'd be able to leave Charlotte with him or one of his sisters for a while.

I remember the first time I left Rachel alone with my mother-in-law. We were living in Maryland and my in-laws were visiting from Alabama. Since we lived far from both our families, Wayne and I had a sliver of opportunity to escape the house together while Rachel was in good hands. I had bought a breast pump, not the cheapest one but not the most expensive either. Sitting in my bathroom, pump cupping my breast, I waited as the machine tugged on my nipple. More waiting, but nothing. I erupted into a blubbering mess of sniffles and tears as I considered that I might never again leave my house, never again get a good night's sleep. It's amazing how quickly one's world turns dark and emotions raw when sleep is scarce.

I learned that the better pumps were worth the money. But they were *a lot* of money. Finding a good one for Sonia on Craigslist became my mission. I made several calls, left messages, waited, and finally found one about forty minutes away. I retrieved it and delivered it to Sonia. It came with many parts. Together we read the directions and figured out what everything was for.

I'm not sure if Sonia ever used the breast pump. I asked her a couple times, and she said she hadn't yet. I decided not to keep asking because I didn't want to make her feel uncomfortable if she had decided it wasn't working for her.

Looking back, I realize that I bought the pump for her, but I did it for *myself* – out of desire to help. I wanted to be needed; I believed that the extent to which I was useful to her was commensurate with my value to her as a friend.

A couple weeks later, I drove to Sonia and Eugene's house after school. When I arrived, Annet and Chantal were lounging on the sofa. Sonia was nursing in the bedroom.

The drawn shades blocked out the daylight. The sisters were half watching *Bridget Jones's Diary*. With the TV blasting, conversation bounced from the movie plot to the women's plans for the future to their predictions of what Charlotte would do with her life. Sonia returned with Charlotte in her arms.

"Yes, she definitely looks like a politician," Annet said. "She's going to be president one day."

"No, she's going to be a doctor. Or maybe a researcher.

Yes, she's going to find the cure for AIDS or cancer, right Sonia?"

"Maybe," Sonia said with a quiet aplomb.

I marveled at the camaraderie these women shared and was a little envious.

After a half hour, it was time for Chantal to leave for class. She was studying at a local college.

"You don't want to be late," Annet said with a stern look toward her younger sister.

"She thinks she's my mother," Chantal responded.

"Well, you need one. What would you do without me? You don't have a car. How would you get to class?" Annet said with a snarky look on her face.

"I would take the bus," she said. "I don't need a mother, but you need a child. You should hurry up and find a husband before it's too late."

"Let's go," Annet said, smiling.

When they left, Sonia went into the kitchen and came back with a bowl of nuts. She held it in front of me.

"Oh, thank you," I said, scooping a small handful.

I was just about to pop one in my mouth when Sonia warned, "No! You don't eat it!"

"What? What is this, Sonia? They're nuts, right?" Sonia let go of her sober expression.

"You're messing with me, Sonia?" At that, we both laughed.

After our snack, I asked Sonia if she wanted to take Charlotte for a walk.

"Right now?"

"Yeah, it's really nice out."

"All right, we can go."

I carried the stroller down two flights of stairs and Sonia followed, holding Charlotte. It was a perfect day to be outside. The sky was bright, and the warm air made it feel like winter was gone for good.

Charlotte was asleep by the time we walked to a nearby playground. Sonia and I sat on a shaded bench. A toddler with a headful of shoulder-length braids climbed to the top of the slide in front of us.

"She's cute," Sonia commented.

"Yes, but I think it's a boy, Sonia."

"No! It's a girl I think."

"Really, Sonia, look. He's wearing jeans and a blue shirt. Besides, his dad has long hair, too."

"No, I don't think so. But you know me, I will just ask." She hollered to the dad standing next to the slide, "Is it a he or a she?"

He took his eyes off his child for a moment. "He."

"Oh, he looks like a girl," Sonia said. I giggled and cringed at the same time. I loved Sonia's courage and confidence, though it did border on rudeness in this particular case. But her boldness was a sign of how far she had come since the day we met. She was now able to show her true colors, and my sweet Sonia indeed had an edge to her. I loved this version of Sonia – Sassy Sonia, I thought!

As we strolled back to the apartment, Sonia confided that she was upset about something. Robert had been talking about moving to Tennessee where one of his brothers lived.

He was going to visit because he thought there might be more opportunities there.

"I don't want to move," Sonia said. "I won't know anybody."

"I know it would be hard to be somewhere without the support of Robert's sisters. I'm sure Robert will realize how important it is to be near family, Sonia." I reached for words to brush away her anxiety.

"Robert is a smart man, Sonia," I said. "A big change like this is not something he's going to take lightly. He just wants to check it out. He won't want to move unless it really is the best decision for all of you."

"I don't know." Sonia said. "Maybe."

"Either way, Sonia, you're going to be fine." She looked at me and I could see her mood begin to lighten. I knew Sonia was worried, but I wasn't. I had a strong feeling the pros and cons of moving would tilt in favor of staying.

"Do you remember when you told me I was going to be a great mother?"

"Yes, of course I do. And I meant it." In this moment, I realized that my words had touched her. I wanted to believe that they also encouraged her, helped her in some small way get to where she was now – a strong, capable mother who was just beginning to discover her true potential. Lord knows she had a hand in carving *me* into a better person.

The breast pump didn't matter anymore, because *my words did.*

21

Saying Good-Bye

Mom spent her last sixteen days in a hospice facility. If you could pick a place to die, this home-turned-hospice was about as nice as they came. Its cozy decor, friendly staff and picture windows overlooking a tree-lined lake could almost make visitors forget they were surrounded by death.

My dad and I stood in the spacious entranceway and watched Mom roll in on a bed navigated by two young men who had transported her from the hospital. Her skin was smooth and pink, her head barely covered by the short, fine hair that was starting to grow back. She sat upright, eyes bright, her expression charged with energy. I let my mood meet hers as I walked to her and hugged her. She smiled as she always did when she saw me, as if there were no cancer between us.

That smile became less reliable in the following weeks, as

she passed through her final stages of life. Her energy and moods were as varied as the sea on each visit. One day she'd be so weak, she could barely speak. The next day she would have the full strength of her voice and be sitting upright in bed. On some days she was angry about dying. On others, she acted as though she was the center of attention at her own party.

I remember calling her one day as I was leaving school. She had been nonresponsive for days. My dad usually picked up the phone, but this time she answered.

"Hi, how aaaare you, Sweetie?" she asked in a perky voice with a strong New England accent. It was the way she'd answered the phone a million times before she was sick.

"I'm fine," I said. "How are you?"

"How do I sound to you?" she responded playfully.

"You sound great, Mom," was all I could think to say.

"That's right," she said. "I'm great!" And she was. For the moment. Her brothers and sisters surrounded her.

The conversations I had with Mom during those two weeks cling to my memory. I am grateful because I can replay the good ones over and over again in my mind like a favorite CD.

One of those memories is of a night I had her all to myself. After the usual entourage of company came and left, Dad and I sat alone with Mom. In her final days, though Mom appeared a million miles away, we acted as if she could hear us. And there were occasional signs she could.

Nesting in a birdhouse just outside Mom's window, two adult finches worked full-time to collect food for their babies.

If we looked closely, we could see the tiny beaks poking out from inside their shelter. The busy new life played out like theater in front of us. When words were hard to find, there was always the activity outside the window to talk about.

On this night, I decided to find some CDs to play for Mom from the vast collection in the upstairs shared living space. I brought them down to her room only to discover that all the CD jackets were empty. Dad and I chuckled, and I went back upstairs, this time checking each one.

I popped in a CD, exchanged a word of dissatisfaction with Dad, and then tried another. And another. This went on for twenty minutes. I wondered if Mom was amused on some level by our struggle to find her the perfect CD.

Instead of going out to dinner that night, I went to the store to buy cheese, crackers, veggies and dip. Dad and I had grown tired of eating at the same restaurants, and we wanted to spend more time with Mom. She was slipping from us, and it seemed only a matter of hours before she'd be completely gone. On the other hand, there were many moments in the past week when we'd felt that way, but Mom kept hanging on. The doctors had said she wouldn't have more than two weeks once she arrived at the hospice. This was day ten and my night to spend with her.

The first thing I did when Dad left was change the television station to a religious channel. A middle-aged man with a booming voice was discussing the importance of faith. Perfect. Maybe I needed to listen, too. So I did. I tried to absorb the message as I watched my mother's chest rise and fall, the only indication that she was still clinging to this world. Mom may have been receding to a new place, but I was utterly present. I felt connected to Sonia who had stood vigil alongside her mother during her final hours.

I scanned the room noting what possessions Mom chose to have close by in her final days: a painting I made of our snow-covered Cape house, a quilt I sewed with messages from loved ones, a flowery blue and green scarf the girls bought her in New York. She was even wearing a Billy Elliot t-shirt we gave her, though it had been cut to accommodate a catheter and morphine tube.

Mom had planned to go to New York with the girls and me. Together we had picked out three shows to see in three days: *The Lion King, Billy Elliott* and *The 25th Annual Putnam County Spelling Bee.* Mom was too sick to go, so we went without her. It was her gift to us. She told my aunt she did it so the girls wouldn't forget her. Really, Mom?

I had read in a brochure that the terminally ill wait until they know their loved ones are all right before they pass. Up to this point, I had tried to be strong for Mom. I wanted to make it easier for her to leave this world – to leave *me.*

This night was different. As I sat on the edge of her bed, studying her expressionless face, I sobbed. I watched her slipping away from me like the tide. It was as if all of the emotion I had stuffed neatly inside myself was seeping out, slowly at first, and then like a river set free by a broken dam. I rested my head on her chest and whispered, "I'm sorry, Mom. I'm blubbering all over you. I can't stand seeing you like this. But pretty soon you'll be rid of this terrible body and you'll be free." I tried to believe the words I spoke. Mom's eyes remained closed, but she mustered a smile. It was as if to say, "I hear you and I know you're right. Everything will be all right." And it was. For the moment.

I had a similar experience with Mom on another occasion. She had been nonresponsive for days, and there was little evidence that she was listening to me. I was alone with her and reminiscing about our family vacations. "Mom," I said, "You have made me into the biggest beach bum ever."

That's when a pleased expression crossed her face, and I knew she could hear me. Of all the sappy comments that came out of my mouth, it was the beach bum image that made Mom happy enough to show me she was listening, when she had energy for nothing else.

I felt like I was leading a double life during those two weeks. At school, hours could pass without a thought in Mom's direction. The business of school grappled for my attention and often won out against my grief. Preparing lessons, teaching classes, grading papers, responding to e-mails – those were the tasks that consumed my energy most of the day.

And then there was the interim math department head position. It was a one-year position (with the possibility of being extended), and it was open to anyone in my department. I thought of applying, but couldn't decide if the position would be a rewarding growth opportunity or a never-ending migraine. In the end, I decided to give it a shot. My interview occurred the second week of Mom's hospice stay.

That Friday, Dad summoned me to the hospital.

"I think it's time," he said. "Everyone is here. You should come if you can."

When I arrived, Mom was bright-eyed and talkative. Her siblings gathered around her, and Mom said her good-byes as if she had accepted her fate.

By morning, Mom's expression and spirit had vanished with the baby finches, now on their own in the world.

On the fifteenth day, the news came. Mom had passed. Alongside the heartache, I felt relieved to know she was rid of pain. Yes, she was free, but the unbearable finality would take time to process. I took deep breaths and tried to let the knowledge seep in.

Dad was eager to give me her things. He showed me her jewelry and I took hold of her gold crucifix ring. Besides her wedding ring, it was the only piece of jewelry Mom never took off. I slipped it onto my ring finger with the same intention.

I was alarmed by my composure over the following week. My behavior felt inappropriate. It would be weeks later when I would let the grief run free.

My daughters remained strong, but the depth of their grief shined through a poem that Rachel had written for the school literary arts magazine. It was profound and raw.

Poem for my Grandma

How does your laughter bubble in the air as
The cancer bubbles inside you?
For now, I will grip your hand, stroking
The fingers that feel brittle beneath mine, as if

To cling to the life that
Threatens to float away. For now,
I will hold back tears, and
Kiss your eggshell skull, and
Listen to the gurgle of your last breaths, when
All I want to do is drown
The hushed whispers, and
Slam the doctors with their bad news
Against the thin hospital wall, just to hear
Your heartbeat pounding like
War drums. I want to
Jab my hand into your chest, and
Grope until I reach
The soft lumps that drain your life, and
Pull them out of you, and
Hold them, like a slimy newborn
Baby and smile, because I
Was the one who saved you.

— Rachel Jenkins

I stopped by Sonia's house to tell her the news in person. It was the same day I learned that I didn't get the department head position.

We sat together on her sofa and shared stories of our mothers. Sonia's eyes were moist with memories. I tried to imagine what it was like for her to lose her mother at such a young age.

I wasn't sure how our traditions surrounding death compared to what Sonia was used to so I explained everything to her.

"I can't go because of Charlotte. But Robert will go to the funeral for us. It's important because you're my friend."

I still have an e-mail that Sonia sent me: "Stay strong. We are together."

PART III

The Receding Tide

22

———

Eugene's Graduation

"Sure I was happy. But mostly I was thinking that I wanted to keep moving, keep going to school." -Eugene

In my mind, I had choreographed Eugene's graduation a jillion times. Filled with pride is how I found myself on the actual day. Even the weather matched the happy occasion – sun shining brightly, air cool and crisp.

Only a couple weeks separated this celebration from Mom's death. Doesn't life have a funny way of handing us the good with the bad, side by side? Maybe it just seems that way. Maybe it's God's plan, to help us get through the dark days. Any sadness I felt stemmed from knowing I wouldn't be giving Mom an earful of details later that day.

The ceremony took place at the Veterans Memorial Auditorium, a vibrant and historic performance hall in the center of Providence. We arrived thirty minutes early to nab good seats. A woman, thirtyish, was collecting tickets but readily let us in without them.

Fresco paintings adorned the high ceilings of the grandiose foyer. I admired the ornate woodwork and felt, for a moment, like I was entering an old opera house.

Inside the auditorium, families swarmed around like bees in a hive. I honed in on four available chairs and raced to them, Lucy style. Luckily, there were more vacant seats nearby for Sonia, Robert, and Charlotte.

Thirty minutes later the crowd settled. The tune of Pomp and Circumstance piped in while beaming black-clad graduates processed down the center aisle. I steadied my gaze on a spot beyond the mass of onlookers to where I had a clear view of each graduate as they passed. I didn't want to miss *my* graduate. When Eugene finally entered my sight, I could almost feel the neurons in my temporal lobe firing. I instinctively called out his name and waved both arms – again, behaving oddly like my mother. My teenage self would have been mortified, but I was grateful for the fleeting connection with Mom.

It took Charlotte six seconds to decide that a cramped auditorium was not where she wanted to be. I happily accompanied her and Sonia to a quiet room downstairs, away from the speeches, crowds and formal rituals. I had had my moment of watching Eugene march to the stage in his cap and gown, and that was enough.

Sonia and I found a bench in a spacious hallway outside the ladies' room.

"I can't believe Eugene is graduating today. I'm so proud of him," I said.

"He's so happy," Sonia said, bouncing Charlotte on her knee. She smiled as if she was thinking of something funny. "He was dancing down the street this morning in his cap and gown." Her smile erupted into a laugh, which infected me.

"Are you kidding? I would have loved to have seen that!"

"Yes, I know." Her expression turned more serious. "In Africa, it cost money to go to school. We didn't have enough money, so Eugene couldn't go."

"And he had to take care of your aunt's store?"

"Yes."

It was no wonder that Eugene prioritized his academics over everything else, including his job and independence.

"He wanted a party for his graduation, but I said 'I don't know.' All the cooking n' cleaning." Sonia frowned.

"I know, but I'm glad you're having a party for him, Sonia. It means a lot to him."

Sonia looked at Charlotte and sighed. "Maybe."

"Have you and Robert talked about getting married?" I said, changing the subject.

"Yes, we're getting married," she said.

"You don't sound excited."

"In Africa, if a man and a woman live together and have children, they're married," she explained. "But here, if you don't have a marriage certificate, you're called a fiancé." Her brows gathered wrinkles of disapproval. "I don't like that. I'm Robert's *wife*."

I flashed back to my mother's funeral. Oddly, it felt inappropriate to introduce Robert to my cousins as Sonia's fiancé or boyfriend. Instinctively, I asked him if it was all right to introduce him as Sonia's husband. Amused by my frankness, he assured me it was. Later, I wondered if I had misstepped. Glad to know I hadn't.

I told Sonia I was happy to no longer be receiving automated messages from Riverdell High School. Because our name was on file as Eugene's emergency contact, we received all messages that went out to parents. We knew when he was absent or tardy, when parent conferences were held, and when his school was cancelled because of snow. One winter morning, a half-woken Rachel heard the message that Eugene's school was closed and assumed it came from Moses Brown. When she shared the good news, we did a little happy dance and went back to sleep. An hour later I replayed the message. A few swear words spilled out of my mouth (even before I was behind the steering wheel); our rest day was over. The girls and I rushed out the door, granola bars in hand, and barely made it to school in time for second period. Sonia laughed as I recounted the story.

After an hour and a half, Sonia and I reunited with our families outside and took some photos.

I walked to the parking garage with Sonia on one side of me, Eugene on the other. Eugene muttered something about his girlfriend. Sonia laughed as if he had told a joke. Eugene grabbed his wallet, yanked out a photo of an attractive Hispanic girl.

"Where is she?" I asked.

"I don't know," he replied, as if I had asked a stupid question. I changed the subject and, before I knew it, we were at our cars.

Wayne, the girls, and I were among the first to arrive at the apartment after the graduation ceremony, followed by Annet and Chantal. The usual group of friends and family came, and there were mounds of food. We sat in the living room, which Sonia worried would be too small. It was a tad crowded, but no one cared. The energy in the room was festive and playful.

Topics changed but the intensity never wavered. At one point, Chantal was arguing with one of Robert's friends about the gender of God.

"Why can't God be a woman?" she repeated in a boisterous tone.

Eugene sat off to the side. He had an iron grip on his diploma.

"He could be, but there is no evidence. The Bible refers to God as Him," one relative chimed in.

"Ah, yes, but who wrote the Bible? Men!" Chantal responded.

"It makes much more sense that God is a woman," Annet agreed.

"Why is that?" Robert asked, smiling as if to egg her on.

"Because God wants peace, not violence and war. Who starts all the wars? Men."

"That's right," Chantal said. "If women were in charge of countries, there would be peace, not war. We need a woman president."

"Yes, maybe you're right," Robert conceded, tempering the energy.

"Hey, Eugene," Wayne switched gears. "Will you miss anything about Riverdell?" Eugene glared at him.

"How about Miss Becky?" I couldn't resist saying, making everyone laugh. Then I handed Eugene a beer for the first time, and held up my own to toast his success. Robert added a comment about Eugene's grip on his diploma and we continued to laugh – even Eugene.

"HAHAHAHAHA I passed my drivin' test. I love you. Miss you. Eugene." Eugene's e-mail made my week because I knew how excited he was to get his license. The next step was to pass the road test within a certain time after completing the written test. He needed to be accompanied by an adult who had a license for at least five years, and Robert qualified. Twice Eugene missed this deadline, which meant he had to retake the written test. He passed two more times. Then, after a two-day driving lesson with Robert, Eugene passed the road test.

He quit his job at CCRI that summer to work full time for Ocean State Job Lot. He saved his money and bought a car. I was proud of him for making good decisions and moving his life in a positive direction. It was time for me to do the same.

23

Return to the Ocean

"The time I came to the Cape, I was so happy. I really hope and wish I can come over there every summer, for real." -Eugene

The summer of 2011 was my season of healing. I was grateful to be spending it on the Cape. I felt in need of the ocean's powers more than ever. It had been a stormy year, one that had washed away my previous notions of security and control. Mom's illness, Sonia's fear, Eugene's detachment – these were situations I was powerless to change. I needed to reconsider my focus, determine what changes I *could* make. I'd start with myself.

And then there was the department head position. Of course, I could've asked my supervisor why I was turned down, but I chose the route of self-pity – convinced myself that I just plain sucked. Besides, the news came on the heels of

Mom's passing and seemed inconsequential next to my grief. But now, self-disparaging thoughts were bouncing around my head like ping pong balls, and I had to get a hold of them.

I got a jumpstart to my attitude adjustment *off-Cape* – in Costa Rica.

My school had acquired a grant for teachers to travel in groups during the summer. In October, I had volunteered for the first expedition, along with two of my female colleagues, Scotte and Betsy. Mom's illness had made the timing of the June trip iffy, but my supervisor assured me I could cancel if needed. This was, after all, my dream trip – a Spanish immersion course near the sea. There would be salsa dancing!

We left in late June, shortly after school let out. As soon as I met up with my friends at the airport, the adventure began. Coming close to missing our flight, Scotte hailed a cart driver at the airport and off we went – hair blowing behind us as we zigzagged past fellow travelers toting kids and luggage. We were laughing.

We spent mornings learning Spanish and afternoons sightseeing. Hours were filled with belly laughter, good beer and bad pronunciation. Betsy was fluent but that didn't stop me and Scotte from practicing Spanish with anyone who'd listen. We made a close friend in our hotelkeeper, José. He called us *Las Tres Princessas* and he treated us as such. Every morning, he amazed us with a breakfast as pleasing to the eye as to the palate. Scotte photographed them. Her enthusiasm was contagious, and I wondered why we hadn't become friends sooner. We had plenty in common, not to mention the same Hanes underwear we both had purchased at Target days before our trip. You learn a lot about a girl when you travel with her.

The summer of 2011 was also the first summer Sonia came to my Cape house. She arrived with Charlotte, Annet, and Chantal in mid-July. I was equally excited and anxious about their visit. I wanted to see them, but somehow my desire for them to have a good time turned into worry about whether or not they would. So much for proper alignment. No doubt it would take time – and practice.

In my usual fashion, I busied myself with preparations to curb my angst. I cleaned the house, stocked the cupboards, cut the grass, did some baking. I even scrubbed the inside of the microwave and swept the leaves off the driveway. How could anything go wrong if I had a clean driveway? I did consider cleaning the refrigerator but stopped myself. A little progress in self-improvement is better than none, no?

The three women showed up late on a Friday night, after getting lost a few times. The trip drained their energy.

The sisters had requested lasagna for dinner. I was happy to oblige, especially since I could make it days before, yank it out of the refrigerator and pop it in the oven when we were ready to eat it.

Lasagna was the first meal I'd cooked for Sonia and Eugene, and Sonia had insisted I show her how to make it. So one day I went to her house, arms overflowing with a glass baking pan and stuffed grocery bag. I brought every ingredient, including the garlic, because I wasn't sure what Sonia kept in her small kitchen. Together we assembled this vegetarian non-cook's version of lasagna using frozen spinach and store-bought tomato sauce. Lasagna was my contribution to meals at their family gatherings because Chantal and Annet raved about it. Eventually, Sonia showed them how to make it as well.

This night called for second helpings. Afterwards, we settled around the fire pit in the rainbow-colored plastic Adirondack chairs.

Night colored the yard like a black paint storm. Trees and a swamp kept neighbors' lights from spilling into our darkness. Not even a lamp was left on in the house, thanks to Sydney the energy miser. I've bruised myself umpteen times walking into furniture in unlit rooms, all for the sake of doing my part to curb global warming.

One dank night in February, I had gone to bed in the sunroom to avoid catching Wayne's cold. The space heater and my handmade quilt – pieced together from old running t-shirts – warmed me as I fell peacefully to sleep. I woke in the middle of the night, freezing, like a glacier had slipped into my bed. The energy elf had struck again. She waited for me to fall asleep, then snuck in and turned the heater off. She figured I wouldn't miss it if I wasn't conscious.

This evening, the dancing amber flames of our fire-starter log kept the cold at bay. Our friends, although exhausted, entertained us with their banter. Rachel and Sydney demonstrated the proper way to toast marshmallows. Annet and Chantal saw this, like everything else, as a competition.

"Oh, I see," Chantal said, watching Rachel's stick rotate over a small flame. "I will make the best one."

"No, you're holding yours too close to the fire," her sister corrected.

"No, this is going to be just right," Chantal insisted.

"So, Chantal," Wayne said as if he wanted to change the subject. "What are you studying? Do you have a major yet?"

"She wants to be a nurse so she can take care of me when I'm old," Annet quipped.

"Maybe you should go to school so you can take care of *me*," Chantal retorted.

"No, I'm too old. You're young. It's your job to take care of your older sister."

"Here you go," Chantal held her long stick up to Annet's face. Her marshmallow was crisp and black.

"Is this how you're going to take care of me? Giving me burnt food?"

"What kind of nurse do you want to be?" Wayne asked, leaning forward. The rich, musky smell of smoke permeated our circle.

"I don't know. Maybe a pediatric nurse."

"That's no good for me," Annet said before devouring her overcooked marshmallow.

I looked over at Sonia who was fading quickly, Charlotte asleep in her arms. I knew she was wiped, but hoped she was happy.

The next morning, we headed to the beach. An earlier miscommunication had led Annet and Chantal to believe they were coming to my Rhode Island house. So instead of bathing suits, they wore long, brilliantly colored African dresses.

We pulled into the tiny parking lot. Unlike other town beaches on the Cape, Brewster beaches had no lifeguards or concession stands. A port-o-john was the only amenity. There were no signs steering tourists to my favorite stretches of sand, tucked in quiet residential neighborhoods. So I wasn't surprised to see several vacant parking spots on this cloudless, midsummer day.

The clear sky gave way to a sharp view of the hook of the Cape off to the right of the horizon. The ocean was a translucent blue-green, calm and seaweed free. We spread our blanket, erected beach chairs and umbrella, and relaxed into our claimed space on the pinkish-white sand.

Charlotte had dibs on the shade, and she slept contentedly as if tucked away in a quiet room. The sun pressed against my skin and I welcomed it at first. It took an hour for the sweat to pool around my temples and the arch of my back. I wiped my forehead and tried to put on sunscreen, but it just swirled around with the sweat. It was time to go in the water.

There are different ways to do this. There's the *all at once like a Band-Aid* method, which is what I did as a kid (usually for money). And there's the *slow torture – but I'm getting acclimated* method. Rachel, Sydney and I took a middle road. In minutes, not seconds, we were submerged.

The ocean reset my body temperature and breathed new life into me. Annet and Chantal joined us, unconcerned that they were wearing dresses. They took turns floating on the Styrofoam noodle, which was almost too small for their womanly bodies. They laughed and argued over who would get the toy.

Eventually Annet gave in to her sister, and then confessed that she didn't know how to swim, but wanted to learn.

"Rachel is an excellent swimmer," I said proudly. "She can teach you."

"Yes, I want to learn how to swim," Annet said.

"OK," Rachel said. "Come here and we'll start with floating on your stomach." As Rachel began her lesson with Annet, I strolled back to my beach chair next to Sonia and, together, we watched the sisters play. In their vibrantly colored dresses of blue and orange, billowing in the water against their dark skin, Annet and Chantal stood out against the monotone seascape.

Annet tried repeatedly to float on her stomach, gritting her teeth in determination. I watched as the sisters grabbed hold of life with every ounce of their beings. They were oblivious to their flowing dresses, heavy and wet, and to the occasional exposure of their full breasts. None of that mattered to them; they were having fun. As I watched from the beach, I realized that I, too, had blocked out all negative thoughts. I was fully engaged in the moment and it felt good.

In the meantime, Wayne headed to the house to retrieve his sunglasses. I asked him to bring back anything he could find that floated. He returned with a narrow pink float that looked like something we had bought at the dollar store. After intense negotiations, Chantal decided to let her sister try it first. Annet threw her wet body onto the float and slid off like a seal. We all laughed. Again, this time with a gentler approach, Annet missed her mark. Two attempts later, she was secure atop her float, gloating, as her sister looked on, holding the noodle, which suddenly seemed like a booby prize.

Later that afternoon, my cousin Amy, her husband Craig and their three children, ages nine, seven, and two, joined us. Amy lived an hour and a half away, and she was the only one who'd drive to the Cape for the day on the spur of the moment. I loved that about her. In my opinion, spontaneous visits by friends were the best kind. Advance preparation wasn't possible, so there was no reason to stress; pressure was off. The bonus in this case was seeing Amy's kids – whom we adored.

By the time my cousin's family arrived, the parking lot was full, and it required some creative shuffling to get everyone to the beach because my car was the only one with a beach sticker. I wondered if my cousin and friends would like each other. If they didn't interact, how could I divide my attention between them? I could feel anxiety seeping into my beach space, but it didn't take over. Something else beat it to the finish line. I'm not sure what to call it, sanity maybe? The realization that I wasn't responsible for other people's happiness clobbered me over the head like a baseball bat. About time.

By three o'clock, sun and sea had sapped our energy. Wayne shuttled everyone back to the house, where we enjoyed watching the two-year-old's fascination with Charlotte. We propped Charlotte's head so we could photograph the two babies sitting on the white rocking chair in the yard. The toddler stared at his new friend, spoke to her and touched her. He didn't mind that his younger friend didn't return his curiosity.

I wanted so badly for Sonia, Annet and Chantal to have a good time. Annet and Chantal were their usual expressive selves, but for some reason I was having trouble reading Sonia.

That afternoon, as Sonia and her sister-in-laws pulled out of the driveway, Sonia said, "Maybe next year we'll come for a week."

I guess I had my answer.

Later that summer, Eugene came to the Cape with his friend, Christopher, who was also from Rwanda. Dimples punctuated Christopher's round face whenever he smiled, which was pretty much all the time. Their visit happened to be the same weekend my Aunt Jayne and Uncle Marty were camping a quarter mile down the road. Marty was my mother's youngest sibling, making him only a few years older than me. As kids, my cousins and I couldn't imagine anyone cooler than Marty. Our teenage uncle with wild hair and red bandana would captivate us with stories of three-fingered Willy and Spider Gates – a local cemetery no sane kid dared venture into. All grown up, Marty was still the best storyteller I knew.

Saturday night was the highlight of Eugene and Christopher's visit. Sydney was at a friend's house and Rachel was working at the nearby ice cream parlor. Jayne, Marty, Wayne, Eugene, Christopher, Ellen (Jayne's sister), and Tom (Ellen's husband) sat around the table in Ellen and Tom's traditional Cape home, tucked away at the end of a nearby cul-de-sac.

We started with the beers – Coors Light and Harpoon IPA. Then Marty mixed some sweet alcoholic concoction in a blender while Jayne kept careful watch over everyone's glasses, refilling as necessary without saying a word. We laughed as Marty told hunting stories in full animation. The free-flowing alcohol and my family's outgoing personalities destroyed any barriers of social etiquette and shyness.

Ellen's teenage boy and twenty-one-year-old daughter bopped in with some friends, then vanished to the deck off the kitchen. After thirty minutes or so, Christopher asked if he and Eugene could go outside to hang with the younger folks – people their own age.

"Of course," I said. I hoped they would all get along and the initial awkwardness, if there was any, would pass quickly.

We soon heard laughter. I looked through the sliding glass door. Eugene was thrashing around the bug zapper – a racquet shaped device that electrocuted mosquitoes on contact – while his new friends cheered him on. More laughter. I could see his teeth glowing in the night.

Yes, Eugene was *smiling*.

Sure, he may have been drunk, but that didn't matter. He was happy. Really happy.

Around nine thirty, someone suggested we go for ice cream and visit Rachel. Jayne was already wearing her Red Sox pajamas.

"You can't go in your pajamas!" Ellen said.

"Why not?"

"Because I know people here."

Jayne scrunched up her face as if she didn't grasp Ellen's point.

Marty and Jayne headed to their truck and the rest of us climbed into Ellen's son's truck. The twenty-somethings crammed themselves into the bed of the truck like commuters on a subway during rush hour. Tom sat in the front, instructing his son to drive slowly along the quiet, ill-lit road.

When we arrived, we unloaded ourselves from the vehicles and packed into the small ice cream store, meant for only a handful of people. Rachel's co-worker looked surprised to see a rush of business at the late hour, and from such a rowdy group. But Rachel perked up when she saw us, like she enjoyed the attention.

That night, as we were driving back from Ellen and Tom's, Eugene said, "I want to come back *here!*" I wasn't sure if he meant Ellen's house, Brewster or the Cape in general. It didn't matter. I was just happy he had a good time.

The following day was cold and windy, but I knew the boys' trip wouldn't be complete without a visit to Nauset Beach – or Big Wave Beach as I still sometimes called it.

Wayne, the girls and I – all wearing sweatshirts – sat in beach chairs, our bodies huddled under towels. Eugene and Christopher swaggered to the water and plunged into the ocean. It didn't matter that the air was chilly, the sky overcast and the water frigid, or that no one else thought it appropriate to be in the water that day. The waves tossed the boys around for a good twenty minutes before they decided to dry off.

Eugene's entire body was shivering as he trekked across the sand, his arms wrapped around his chest as if he could warm himself. We handed him an extra sweatshirt and towel, and he covered himself as quickly as his shaking hands could manage. His teeth rattled.

Meanwhile, Christopher sauntered over and carefully smoothed his towel on the cool sand. He spread himself, as if sunbathing on a tropical island.

"You're not cold?" I asked for my own amusement.

"No, I don't get cold," he said with all of us staring at him. Eugene was still shaking.

Dad took tiny but deliberate steps toward coping with Mom's death. Watching him made me realize that I was the daughter of *two* courageous parents.

It started with the purging – almost immediately after Mom died. It continued for months. Kitchen utensils, crock-pots, hand-made quilts – it all had to go. To the Salvation Army, to friends, to relatives. It didn't matter. Dad explained that he was doing it for me, so I wouldn't be bothered having to go through it all when he died. I claimed Mom's Cape Cod sweatshirts. My daughters inherited her Cape Cod jewelry. I had no idea she had such a collection. Seeing, touching, smelling all of these possessions soothed me, made me feel close to Mom.

I discovered that Mom was a bit of a hoarder. This was ironic considering she had always complained about Mémère keeping stuff she didn't need. When Dad retired, he kept the house impeccable while Mom was working so no one would have guessed their fourteen-hundred-square-foot home contained at least two of everything: two crockpots, two coffee pots, three bread makers, hundreds of cookbooks. And it all had to go. Even the family recipes.

In the process of going through Mom's things, Dad found numerous lists she had written, and they came in quite handy. Among them were a list of steps for turning on the computer, a list of people to send Christmas cards to, and a list of people's birthdays and anniversaries, along with the amount of money she had sent them. My dad referred to those lists often, but eventually revised them, made them his own.

"I'm not sending Julie and Barbara Christmas cards next year," he said one day. "No, the hell with them. They weren't there for your mother when she was sick." And that was that.

Everything changed when Mom died. But then again, some things *needed* to change. I made new promises to myself as another summer slid into autumn. This time I felt more capable of keeping them, of not letting them blow away with the wind when I crossed the Sagamore Bridge.

I vowed to hold at bay the worrisome thoughts that popped into my head. I would smile more and mean it. I would take time to be with nature on a regular basis – even in the dead of winter – so that she could calm my nerves, buoy my spirit long after summer was over.

I decided that if I wanted to live more in the moment, I needed to be open to the unexpected. I would fight my tendencies to always be in control so that I might open a door for something new, something that would catch me off guard like a summer storm and wash me away if only for a minute.

It was easy in Costa Rica, but life's routines make this a challenging promise to keep. I was up for the challenge.

And I would cherish those moments, let them seep into my relationships with family and friends, with Sonia and Eugene.

Sonia and Eugene.

What a perfect example. I opened the door to my heart and let their affection seep in, albeit ever so slowly. They, too, have taught me the gift of being present – of being open to finding joy in the most unexpected places.

24

——

Marriage

"Robert supports me so much, even when I'm childish. When he first proposed to me in front of his two sisters, I was so nervous. I didn't say anything. Robert put the ring in my hand and closed it. Then we both laughed. He didn't get mad because he knows me, knows how I am." -Sonia

Sonia and Robert were married in the fall of 2011, on an overcast, chilly day. Sonia had told me the celebration would begin at two o'clock at her house, after she and Robert returned from the courthouse.

"I was going to ask you to be my sponsor," she said, explaining why my presence wasn't needed at the courthouse. "But you didn't pick up the phone when I called, and I figured you were busy. So, I asked another friend." I knew Sonia meant she didn't want to impose. But the thought that

I *could have been there* if I had been home when she called or stayed in better touch with her weighed on my heart. Sonia didn't realize that it would have been an honor to be there with her – not a burden.

The girls were still in separate corners of the house getting ready at two o'clock. Wayne was taking clothes out of the dryer.

I got grouchy.

"We're going to be late! It's so rude!" I said as my family moseyed to the car. I didn't understand why everyone was so complacent.

"Don't worry, Hon," Wayne soothed. "It's African time. They don't really want us there at two."

While I understood his reasoning, I was sure that Sonia knew me well enough at this point to tell me the actual time she wanted us to arrive, so I couldn't help but feel unsettled during the twenty-minute car ride to their house.

While we were at the Cape, Robert and Sonia had moved again. This time I was able to see their apartment for the first time once everything was unpacked and put in its proper place. Their new place was closer to Annet and Chantal's house, and only a couple blocks from Eugene, who had moved back into his old apartment with Emmanuel.

It was three o'clock when we walked in the door and were greeted by Robert's family. They had already eaten!

"What happened?" Annet asked. I scrunched my lips, wondering how much I should protect the husband I was furious with. I couldn't help myself.

"It's *his* fault. He said, 'Don't worry, it's African time!'" My friends' laughter wiped away my tension. Sure, I may have let my fury leak out at my husband's expense, but at least I didn't feel the need to wear that fake smile!

25

Charlotte's Birthday

"I was excited but worried where everyone would sit. But then I thought maybe the kids could all just sit on the stairs." -Sonia

Charlotte's first birthday party was on her actual birthday, which fell dead center in the middle of a workweek in January – and squarely in the middle of my hibernation period, my time-out season of life. As soon as I came home from school, I'd change into my faded blue lobster pajamas, throw together a resemblance of dinner, then curl up on my sofa with a cup of red rooibos tea. I'd watch trash TV and tuck myself away by nine o'clock. Venturing out in the evening this time of year, especially in the middle of the week, was way outside my introverted hibernating comfort zone. If the invitation had come from anyone else, I'd have thought of a little white lie to secure an evening with my lobster pajamas and Ryan Seacrest. But how could I miss Charlotte's first birthday party?

Eugene was working that evening, and I was disappointed he wasn't able to come to the party. I hadn't seen him in a while and I missed the boy. His schedule was full, and now that he and Sonia weren't living together, I saw less of him. I'd e-mail him when I was planning to visit Sonia, and sometimes he'd meet me there. More often, he was at school or work or just plain exhausted. I was proud of him for the life he was building.

Sonia had told us the party was at four o'clock, but we didn't realize she had told us the "African time." You'd think we'd have resolved this issue by now.

The frigid air clung to me for long minutes after arriving at Sonia's apartment. Being the first to arrive, I once again found myself in my mother's shoes.

Three recent photographs of Sonia, Robert and Charlotte – professionally done – adorned the living room walls. The place was immaculate. Not even a stray toy blemished the floor. My stomach clenched in hunger as I ingested the savory aroma of Annet's rice floating in from the kitchen. She and Sonia were busying themselves with final food preparations.

Rachel sat on the floor with Charlotte and helped her open her birthday gift. Robert watched with a father's adoration as Charlotte pushed the red and green buttons on her new toy and danced to the music.

Wayne asked Robert about his brother who was studying

at Princeton. Robert explained that his brother was in Africa doing research, and he planned to visit their younger brother whom they hadn't seen in fifteen years.

"If you've only been here for five years, why is it you haven't seen your brother in fifteen?" I had to ask. Being a math teacher, it was important that all the numbers added up. Annet explained that their brother went missing during the war, and he didn't find his way back until years later, after many family members had already come to the United States. They spoke without changing their tone or expression, as if this sort of thing happened all the time. This was how it was with Robert's family. They didn't talk at length about themselves. Rather, they revealed bits of their eventful lives as they came up naturally in conversations – without drama or pretense.

After an hour, Sonia began apologizing for the delay. I felt guilty that she could read our impatience. Rachel and Sydney had a lot of homework, as usual, and Sydney was unable to conceal her discontent in having to wait so long for the party to start. She was a list person, and I suspected she was running through her head all the items on her "to do" list for that evening: finish homework, make tomorrow's lunch, take shower, feed dog and chickens. (Mom would've been proud.)

Relief came when guests trickled in. Before long, all the seats in Sonia's small living room were occupied, and people made themselves comfortable on the floor. Some women wore traditional African dresses, and one shy boy, about four, was dressed in an oversized suit. There were no presents, just good company and lots of well wishes.

When it was time to eat, as if she had done this countless times, Sonia took care of the children first. She organized them two by two on the stairway leading up to the bedrooms. They sat with plates on laps as Sonia supervised them, making sure they didn't go upstairs or make a mess. In that moment, I saw a new Sonia. She was calm and confident, firm and gentle at the same time. Motherhood came naturally to her.

In the main area that served as both a living and dining room, adults helped themselves to chicken, pizza, and fries spread on the kitchen counter. Annet and Chantal took turns entertaining the birthday girl.

Sonia returned from the stairwell and chatted with guests, though she kept returning to check on the children. A competent and graceful Sonia had stepped into the role of hostess. I couldn't help but picture her the way she was when I first met her three short years ago. The contrast was remarkable. I was looking at a strong, mature and loving mother, wife, sister and friend. I wondered if she saw herself the same way I did. It was that moment when I decided to write a book about Eugene and Sonia.

26

Moving On

"Hahaha. So you say you want to write a book? That's great. I will just keep trying to be the man that I am." -Eugene

A month after Charlotte's birthday, I received an e-mail explaining that the math department position was again open. I pushed aside tangled emotions and listened to the voice of reason telling me to give it another go. Sure, embarrassment and humiliation would befall me if I applied and didn't get the position *twice*. But I knew I hadn't really tried the first time. During the interview, my heart and mind were with Mom and my family. This time would be different, and I knew it. As I thought about what I'd say, sitting on the edge of my bed looking into my mirror, I forced myself to see my mother in the bottom half of my face. I always thought I looked more like Dad, but in that moment I realized I had

Mom's cheeks, mouth, and chin. If I had her physical features, I thought, maybe I also had her courage.

I thought of the courage it took for Eugene and Sonia to survive their past, come to the U.S. and start a new life by themselves. Applying for a promotion was nothing compared to the challenges Eugene and Sonia had faced. Or Mom and Dad. Yes, I had solid role models. No excuses.

One brisk afternoon in late February, I spoke with Sonia about my decision to reapply. She was sitting on her sofa with the TV on. I was on the floor with Charlotte, building a tower of blocks. I finally gave voice to the platoon of doubts hiding out in my head. What if I didn't get the job? What if I *did*?

"You should do it," she encouraged with no uncertainty in her voice. "You can do it. Yes, you should apply."

Sonia's words surprised me. She wished I had more time for her as it was. Comments such as, *I know you're busy, but don't forget about me* (always said with a smile) had me leaving her apartment with a mountain of guilt on a regular basis. I, too, wished I didn't have as many demands on my time, that I could spend more hours with her.

"What if I don't get it?" I said. "That would be embarrassing, right? And if I do, well, that doesn't mean I'd be good at it or that I'd even like it."

"But you should try, and don't worry so much. No matter what, everything will be OK."

"Really?" Charlotte placed a block on top of our two-foot structure. It crumbled to the floor, making her giggle.

"That's what you always tell me," she said. "You always

say 'everything is going to be OK.'" And she was right; I did always tell her that. And I always meant it.

The four weeks leading up to spring break seemed to crawl, but I was finally free of school obligations and comfortably settled on our preferred side of the Sagamore Bridge. Tension drained from my body like the water drains from the Brewster flats. I took long walks on the beach, watched as many sunsets as possible, and visited the seals in Chatham Harbor, devouring as much of the sights, smells, and sounds of the ocean as my senses could take in. Convinced of the healing properties of this place, I gathered these moments like a squirrel preparing for a long winter. I had two and a half months of school left, and I had to try to make the nourishment of the sea last until I returned.

I thought of Robert's family and all they had endured. Perhaps it was *because* of what they had weathered that they were able to cherish every moment with each other, laugh so easily. Maybe I could learn a lesson from them. Maybe just showing up was the first step to being present. Cooking utensils, fans, breast pump – sure, these were nice things to have and I'm glad I was able to provide them for Sonia and Eugene. But that's not what made them like me, accept me as their friend. No, that was much simpler. It was only a matter of being there for them over time, as I knew I would, as *Wayne* knew I would that first outing to the beach. And it was a matter of letting them be there *for me*. Because the truth was, we needed each other.

I thought about what prompted this journey – the woman

at Amos House who never learned my name – and how unsatisfying that work was because of the anonymity. It reminded me of my year in Rochester, and how lonely I was to be surrounded by mere acquaintances. I thought about how familiar I now felt with Eugene and Sonia, how far we'd come since that first day at the Institute. Time's patient hand had stripped away the protective armor and revealed our true selves to one other. This was the real gift of friendship. These were my thoughts as I psychologically prepared myself to leave my safe haven.

I returned to Rhode Island a day ahead of my family so I'd have time to visit Sonia and Eugene. I called ahead and planned to visit Eugene at his apartment first, then make the quarter-mile drive to Sonia's apartment.

Eugene greeted me at the door. I hugged him and followed him to the top of the stairs to his living room. I glanced around his apartment; nothing stood out of place. No dirty dishes in the sink, no clutter on his countertop, not one piece of paper on the coffee table. Three chairs in perfect alignment sat opposite his sofa, between them a large flat-screen TV. We sat next to each other on the couch, and I asked him how he was doing and filled him in on our lives. I told him about Rachel's search for a summer job, and how nervous she was about her first interview. I knew her stress would amuse him. To him, it was a child's fear. He was so beyond that now.

I had many questions for him. How was he doing at the community college? Had the public school adequately prepared him? He said it had, and he assured me that school was going fine. We reflected on his days at Riverdell.

"I remember that you said there were gangs at some of the other schools. Were there gangs at Riverdell?"

"Yes," he said tightening his forehead, as if I should have known the answer. "I got into a fight once." Eugene looked me in the eye. He had looked me in the eye before, but this time was different: He didn't look away afterwards. His eyes latched onto mine, and he didn't resist. In that moment, I was looking at a grown-up version of the boy I had met at the Institute three years earlier, and a surge of pride welled up inside me.

"Really? What happened?"

"Someone took my friend's iPod, so I hit him."

"Did you get hurt?"

"Yeah, a bit. There were four of us and ten of them."

"Four of you against ten of them?"

"Four of us against, maybe seven of them." I was not surprised that Eugene would engage in a fight over his friend's iPod. What I was surprised by was the way he volunteered the information and spoke so openly about it.

I was on a roll, so I continued to probe, eventually getting to his childhood and time in Zambia.

"I was in a prison there, you know." Eugene continued to maintain eye contact with me as he explained how he was put in prison for not having the proper paperwork once he emigrated from Rwanda to Zambia. He was taking care of his aunt's store and his inability to speak the native language made him stand out as a foreigner. He was imprisoned for a few months after his aunt had already left the country. And for reasons he didn't understand, was eventually let go.

My phone rang as Eugene was talking. I answered because only a few people knew my cell number; it could've been an emergency.

The familiar voice on the other end was Sonia's. "I just wanted to make sure you were still coming today, Chris," she said.

"Yes, I'm at Eugene's right now. I'll be over in a little while."

"Oh, all right. It's such a nice day. I thought maybe you changed your mind and decided to go to the beach." She laughed as she said this.

"No, Sonia, I'm still coming." Her beach comment shined a spotlight on how close we'd become. *She gets me in a way many others don't.*

The doorbell buzzed. Eugene walked downstairs and came back with a large box.

"It's my camera." He tore open the carton and I looked on with curiosity. It was a Canon handheld camcorder.

"Wow, that's nice. I hope you're planning to record your niece." I had no idea what else he would use the camera for.

I told Eugene he'd have to visit us on the Cape over the summer.

"I can't wait!" he said.

After an hour, I invited Eugene to go to Sonia's with me, but he told me he had to work. I was surprised because he hadn't mentioned it beforehand.

I headed to Sonia's house, wrapped in the satisfaction of finally dismantling Eugene's protective wall.

"Eugene is so much more mature and grown up!" I said

when we were sitting in her living room. "I guess it's been a while since I've spent time alone with him. I know he's quiet in groups, but I still feel like he's changed since he left high school." Sonia laughed gently as she often did when I got animated. But she agreed.

Then she told a story of a recent exchange she'd had with Eugene. Their older brother had called Sonia from Africa, asking for a hundred dollars to bring his sick daughter to the hospital. The older brother never asked Eugene for money because he was the youngest. But Sonia had often sent money to her brother in Rwanda, and she was struggling to pay her tuition bill. She decided to ask Eugene for help. In the past, Eugene would have scoffed at the idea of helping his brother, so Sonia had no expectations.

Eugene wrote a check on the spot.

He told her he had all kinds of comforts and his poor brother was still struggling in Africa. He even said he was going to try to be more careful with his money and give up some of his luxuries so he would be able to continue to help his brother.

I pictured Eugene's new camera and chuckled to myself. It didn't taint my respect or affection for the boy. He had earned the darn thing, though I still wondered what he was planning to use it for.

"Sometimes he'll go shopping with me and buy me gifts," Sonia added, enjoying herself. "The last time we went, he told me to pick something out for myself, but I felt bad. So I just got new shoes. They were twenty dollars." She added,

"Sometimes I invite him over for dinner and he says, 'No, I'm cooking!'"

Somehow our discussion about food turned into one about restaurants. I mentioned that one of my favorite restaurants, an inexpensive Asian restaurant, was in her neighborhood. I had taken her there a long time ago, but she hadn't been impressed.

"What is your favorite restaurant, Sonia?" I asked.

"Olive Garden," she said definitively. "I don't go often. Maybe for my birthday Robert will take me. But it's my favorite restaurant."

"I like Olive Garden, too," I said. I didn't think Sonia remembered that Olive Garden was the restaurant we took her and Eugene to the first winter they were in the U.S. Hearing it was now her favorite pleased me.

"How's your new class going?" I said, switching subjects. Sonia had re-enrolled at the community college. Because she had failed a class when she discovered she was pregnant, she needed to pass a course in order to again be eligible for financial aid. There was a lot riding on her performance. A misunderstanding about her tuition payment resulted in Sonia missing a couple classes and losing a spot in the original instructor's class; she'd continue with a new teacher with fewer students.

"I don't like my new teacher," she said. "The first one was good. She cared. She was just like you." I paused to digest the huge compliment she gifted me.

It was ironic that she showed me her writing textbook on the day I stopped by to tell her I wanted to write a book about our friendship. I skimmed her textbook so I could summarize each section for her. When I finished explaining how to write a good paragraph and topic sentence, she pulled her completed homework assignment out of a blue folder: two paragraphs on Rwanda's economy. Although it included spelling and grammatical errors, her paper reflected a clear understanding of how to write a paragraph. The first one described the poverty of Rwanda at the time she lived there, citing specific examples. The second paragraph explained how Rwanda had changed and had become more technologically advanced over the last decade. My positive feedback surprised her.

That's when I told Sonia about wanting to write a book. Mainly I wanted her permission before I invested a mountain of time.

"That's fine. But, do you have the time to write a book?" she asked, making me wonder if our roles had reversed.

As I played with Charlotte on the living room floor, Sonia went to the kitchen and came back with a grilled cheese sandwich. She handed me the plate.

"Do you remember when you showed me how to make this?" she asked.

"Of course," I answered. I felt like I remembered every moment we shared together. As we chatted, Sonia made a comment about how I looked much healthier than I did a year ago.

"Do you remember when we took Charlotte for a walk to the park?" she asked.

"Yeah, I remember."

"You looked too skinny. I think it was because you were

so stressed about your mom." Her honesty and perceptiveness reflected the depth of our friendship, and I wondered, *when did our relationship change?* I knew it had been a gradual metamorphosis, and I was grateful for it and certain our lives would forever be connected.

While we were talking, Sonia scooped Charlotte up and wrapped her in a sturdy cotton fabric of blazing reds and oranges. She secured the baby to her small frame in about ten seconds.

"Sonia, we pay a lot of money for baby front packs, backpacks, you name it. And I could never get my kids in one without another person helping me. You just did the same thing like it was nothing!"

"This is how we do it in my country," she said with humor.

Charlotte's eyelids fluttered as she drifted to sleep.

"I can't believe she's asleep already," I said.

"She was so tired. I kept her up for you." Sonia knew how disappointed I would be if Charlotte slept through my visit.

"I'll go put her in her crib," she said and disappeared for a few minutes.

When she returned, Sonia told me she was looking for a part-time job to help make ends meet. She was frustrated because she had forgotten how to send her resume electronically.

"When Robert gets home, I try to ask him, but he is too tired. He just tells me that I'm doing it wrong." Sonia is quick to defend Robert. "He is not pushing me, though. He says, 'why are you trying so hard? Don't worry. You'll find something.'"

"I can show you how to cut and paste your resume, Sonia. I sent it to you in an e-mail."

Sonia looked embarrassed. "Oh, I didn't know. I was just copying my resume every time. It took me two hours to do one job application." She was half laughing as she said this.

She sat next to me on her living room floor, both of us leaning against the sofa. With the laptop propped on my thighs, I showed her how to cut and paste her resume.

"I can't believe you typed out your resume for every application, Sonia!"

"I know. It's crazy!" she said.

We looked at each other and giggled like sisters.

Epilogue

"Stop! Stop!" Abood barks into his cell phone, looking out his rearview mirror. He pulls the International Institute van to the side of the bustling street. I'm not sure what's happening. Perched high in the passenger seat next to him, I see a woman's scowling face as she maneuvers her gray Honda around our twelve-person van. She's pissed. But Abood's on a mission. I look at Rachel in the back seat and we both laugh as Abood carries on with the yelling, switching between English and some other language. Abood's grimace tells me we shouldn't be laughing, but I can't help myself.

"Stop! Turn around! Kito!" Then some words I don't understand.

After about five minutes, a young man with a friendly grin slides open the van door, sits next to Rachel. We introduce ourselves.

"Kito! What does stop mean?" Abood is still shouting. Kito draws an octagon with his hands.

"He knows what stop means for a car, but not for a person," Abood says to me, still exasperated.

"Stop for a person, Kito!" He puts his hands up as some sort of helpful gesture, like he is trying to stop something from hitting him in the face.

I try to help by walking my fingers across my hand, then stopping. Kito smiles and nods, but I'm not sure he really understands. He's probably trying to stop the nonsense. The energy in the van is charged, although there are only four of us: Rachel, Abood, Kito and me.

Rachel and I are on spring break. It's her senior year. I received an e-mail from the International Institute asking for volunteers to help set up apartments for new arrivals. This was the day Rachel and I agreed to help, and we're on our way to an apartment that will soon be home to a family of nine.

"I'm sending Kito with you," Abood explains. "You might need help moving furniture, and he has no appointments today. He wants to start taking classes right away, but there are things you have to do when you first arrive."

"How long has he been here?"

"Two weeks. He's alone, like I was when I came here seven years ago." Abood looks at me, half smiling. "And I'm *still* single."

"Where are you from?" I ask Kito.

"Congo."

"It's not good to be alone too long, so it's better that he's with you," Abood says to me.

We pull into a small lot behind a three-story apartment building near the highway. Hand-drawn lines designate the parking spaces. A large dumpster sits in the corner of the property.

Abood plans to show us what to do, then bring me back to the Institute to get my car so he won't have to pick us up. I realize now that we could have saved time by driving separately in the first place. But Abood's very concerned about me getting lost, although I assure him I'm familiar with the neighborhood; Sonia and Eugene live a couple blocks away. Abood makes Kito write his address on a scrap of paper, to be sure he can.

Rachel, Kito and I spend the morning putting up a shower curtain, arranging furniture, and unpacking kitchenware in the small third-floor apartment. It looks much like Sonia and Eugene's first apartment, but with one more bedroom. It's hard to imagine a family of nine living here. Most of the items – furniture, plates, clothes – are donated. A scratched, wooden framed mirror with a wire on the back sits on the floor. I don't see a place to hang it, so I leave it there. An assortment of ten chairs and two small sofas fill two of the rooms, but one is meant to be a bedroom I think. A black and white floral comforter, with large bold print, covers one of the beds. It looks new, and it stands out against the rest of the décor, which time and use have faded.

We unpack a large cardboard box, unwrap plates, cups, and bowls, and admire the blue and gold ceramic pieces as we place them on the counter. I think a wealthy family from the East Side must have donated them. Luck of the draw, really, in terms of who gets what.

Kito lifts a large glass vase to his mouth and pretends to drink from it.

"This one is Rachel's." He says, making us laugh.

When we finish, we head to my car, and I tell Kito about our friends who live nearby.

"I'm visiting Sonia tomorrow, but I'm going to call her now, see if she's home. Maybe you can meet her."

"OK," Kito says.

"Hi, Sonia. Where are you?" I say into my cell phone.

"I'm at Annet and Chantal's."

"I was wondering if I could stop by."

"I have an appointment at one o'clock," she informs.

"All right. I'll see you tomorrow then."

As we pull out of the driveway, I decide to take my chances that Annet and Chantal are still home. How great would it be if I could bond them to Kito, gift him with their friendship. As if it were that easy. *Tah, dah! Here you go, Kito – two amazing women who have gone through struggles like you have, and they live only a few blocks away.*

No, friendship can't be forced. It must be nurtured, cared for over time, allowing fate and effort to join hands. I figure if I make the effort on Kito's behalf, fate will take it from there.

In a few minutes, I'm knocking on Annet's door. Her younger brother, the newest arrival from Africa, peers through the curtain to see our faces before letting us in. He's talking on the phone.

"Annet and Chantal just left," he tells me, and I apologize for the intrusion.

My plan to introduce Kito to my African friends is a bust. For now. There'll be other opportunities, I'm sure.

Rachel puts Kito's address into the GPS and we find our way to his apartment in a rundown neighborhood, a couple miles from the International Institute. Good thing we had Wayne's GPS because Kito wouldn't have been able to direct us, not yet. Rachel plugs our phone numbers in his cell phone, and he writes his e-mail address, phone number, and name on a piece of paper. I step out of the car to hug him good-bye.

"Now you have two more friends in the U.S.," I say.

"Yes. That is good," he says.

That night he sends Rachel a text: *Goodnight Chris and Rachel.*

Kito keeps popping into my thoughts over the next couple days: his charming smile, his easy laugh, the twinkle in his eye. I picture him in his shabby apartment with his unfamiliar roommate. I want to see him again and soon. I picture myself rushing to his apartment, checking his cupboards, making a list of items I can provide for him. I catch myself and remember the lessons I learned from Eugene and Sonia. Yes, I will see this boy again, but I won't rush in – bringing all that anxiety with me. Showing up is all that matters. I don't need to win him over; we're already friends.

Four days later, Sunday evening, the four of us pick Kito up from his new home and take him to a small independent movie theater near Moses Brown. Only a few miles from his apartment, the bustling college neighborhood is a dramatic change from what he has recently grown used to. We arrive early, and Rachel sits next to Kito. She seems to be his favorite anyway. Kito keeps the hood of his gray sweatshirt pulled over his head.

An exhausted Rachel is not bubbling with conversation this evening. A Darius Rucker concert Friday night kept us all up past our bedtimes, including Eugene. (It was Eugene's first concert.) Rachel spent the previous night at a friend's house. Teenage girl sleepovers never end with a good night's sleep. As I sit in the movie theater, three seats from Kito, I recognize the loud silence in our row. Anxiety rushes in, but something else arrives first. Perspective. I breathe, and allow myself to relax in the silence. It feels good. It will take time to work out all the kinks in my DNA, but I commit to the effort.

We exit the theater, after watching a fast-paced quirky movie with random scenes of violence that Kito had no chance in hell of understanding. "I think this is a very good place," he says.

I have no idea if he means the movie theater, Providence, the hip East Side neighborhood. Doesn't matter. He just paid me for the ticket one hundred times over.

We walk down the busy street to our car, and Kito stops in front of a small bagel shop.

"I know someone," he says, looking through the glass storefront.

I holler to my family, several yards away, "Wait! Kito sees someone he knows." But I find it hard to believe. I've been teaching a block from here for fifteen years, and the girls have been going to school in this neighborhood their whole lives. But Kito runs into someone *he* knows?

A woman in her twenties with straight brown hair steps outside to greet him.

"Jennifer!" he says.

"Hi," she responds, looking confused to see her new refugee client walking down Thayer Street with a white family.

She introduces herself as the new employment coordinator at the International Institute. "Are you a volunteer?" she asks me.

"No, we're Kito's friends." I know I'm being mysterious but it's the truth. We're not volunteers. We're not even doing this out of the goodness of our hearts. We met someone who captivated us, and we wanted to spend time with him. Isn't that how friendships are born? And they only survive to the extent that they're mutually beneficial. No doubt in my mind that whatever this one morphs into, I'll be the winner. I already am.

On the drive back to Kito's house, we grill him. We learn that he's twenty-five years old, he used to work as a welder, and he speaks Swahili (as does Robert's family). His ESL class starts the following day, and he has his bus ticket to get there. He wants to find a job, any job, and he wants to find it "fast, fast."

When we arrive at his apartment, Kito steps out of the car, pokes his head back in to speak to us.

"You are my family now," he says, then lets out a giggle. "I am your first born." The girls and I laugh, and I feel my heart fill with affection.

But feelings of guilt temper my excitement over the next week. Would Eugene and Sonia feel like they're being replaced if they knew I was developing a relationship with another refugee?

As if!

While I think about — I mean obsess over — this question, clarity and perspective hit me over the head like a jetty rock. Sonia and Eugene *are the reason* I'm able to step into this new relationship so easily. Two hours after meeting Kito, I gave him my phone number and e-mail address. Would I have done that if I hadn't developed a strong bond with Sonia and Eugene? Doubtful. No, I'm not afraid to plop myself into Kito's life, to be his friend. In fact, I'm eager, and that's a testament to the impact Eugene and Sonia have had on my life! It suddenly makes sense, like the puzzle pieces of my relationship with Eugene and Sonia fitting together, and so perfectly.

My relationship with Eugene and Sonia was planned, sort of, though I never imagined how important they'd become to me. Kito's was unexpected, a result of opening myself up to new possibilities. He was my summer storm.

The following week I go to Sonia's house to get her feedback on parts of my manuscript.

"Right here, it's not clear if you're talking about my aunt or my mother," she says.

I read the sentence. She's spot on.

"You're right, Sonia. I'll fix that."

She giggles. "Now I'm editing *your* writing?"

Before I respond, my phone rings. I stumble to find it in my purse and manage to answer it before it goes to voice-mail. It's Kito. I can't really understand what he's saying. The only words I catch are "Rachel" and "Facebook." We recently friended each other, but it took several days for me to find him on Facebook. He wrote his name out neatly enough, but didn't leave any spaces. Who would have guessed that his middle name – or initials – consisted of two letters. African names, aye yai yai.

"That was Kito," I tell Sonia, who is still studying my manuscript.

"How is the new boy?" she asks.

"Good," I say, smiling, "I think he's good."

About the Book

Eugene and Sonia impacted my life in ways I couldn't have imagined. Their courage, resilience and faith inspired me to write this book; it's my way of sharing with others the gift of their friendship and lessons they've taught me during the three years these pages cover.

The quotes at the beginning of each chapter come from conversations that took place after these events took place.

I changed some names and personal details in order to protect the privacy of individuals. I replaced Sonia's husband and his family with fictional characters to fully protect their privacy. However, I did so in a way that does not affect the heart of the story. My students and advisees are not real, but rather composites of students I've had.

I condensed the time frame in a few instances for the sake of the story (e.g. I combined events that happened on two separate trips to the beach into one scene).

The core of the story – my reflections and experiences – is real, subject only to the limitations of memory.

Acknowledgments

I am in debt to more people than I could possibly name. However, there are some folks I must mention because this book simply would not exist without their help. First, I want to express my gratitude to Marcie Hershman, Caroline Leavitt, and Stephanie Kaye Turner for their fabulous editing; Respect, thanks, and admiration go to Debbie Phipps for her ongoing friendship and guidance – not to mention her unwavering optimism; My cousin, Amy Bartelloni, was invaluable as a writer and friend; I am thankful to Jane Komarov, who generously helped me put the final touches on my manuscript and allowed me to vent on a regular basis while walking our dogs on Cape Cod; I am deeply grateful to my friend and partner in crime, Valerie O'Connor, for always having my back and not allowing me to take myself too seriously; Love and adoration go to Sonia and Eugene – my inspiration for writing this book. I'll be eternally grateful that their names were the ones I chose from the bulletin board; Love and thanks from the bottom of my heart to Dad for bringing me to the Cape every summer, and to my first read-ers, Rachel and Sydney. They gave me the courage to share my voice with the world; and thank you doesn't seem adequate enough for my husband, Wayne, who never doubted that I would finish this book. Finally, thank you to all my friends and family who saw less of me during the three years I dedicated to writing this story. Love to all.

22722741R00166